What Others Say

"What a delightful piece of work Chuck Lund has created! I loved reading it and am thrilled by the wonderful insights and pieces of advice he wove into his story. How wonderful it would be if every man – who was contemplating remarriage or a first marriage to a woman with children – would read his book from cover to cover. Not just once but several times in order to avoid missing a critical morsel."

Margorie Engel, MBA Ph.D.
President & CEO
Stepfamily Association of America

"I enjoyed reading 'The Wedding Was Great, but...' and found it insightful, witty, and very useful for those entering the land-mined world of stepfamilies. The author's openness is painfully refreshing and evokes strong memories of similar situations and reactions that were part of my experience in my stepfamily. Men will identify with the message; women will learn why men react as they do. This is a fine example of a couple working from different perspectives and forming a strong bond and creating a wonderful family."

Robert Klopfer, LCSW
Co-Director, Stepping Stones Counseling Center
Ridgewood, NJ
www.stepfamilies.com

"This book is a 'must read' for stepfathers! I will be recommending it to the stepfathers I encounter. This book is an inspiration for any stepfather who needs encouragement and positive advice. What I truly loved is how the author and his wife worked together as a team for the success of their stepfamily.

Marion M. Summers, M.Ed.
Stepfamily Association of America

" 'The Wedding Was Great, but..' is a truthful and courageous account of one man's journey through stepfamily life. This book underscores how living in a stepfamily can promote individual growth, a notion that is hard to fathom for many just beginning this journey. I applaud the integration of clinical and therapeutic findings with his account of dealing with the myriad of issues in a stepfamily. I have been looking for a stepfamily book that speaks to the male perspective and also speaks to the rewards of hanging in there for the long haul. This is it and I will heartily recommend this book to my clients and colleagues."

Chris Wucherer MSW ACSW
Stepfamily Solutions
http://www.stepfamilysolutions.net

"The central theme of this book is embodied in the sentence on page 26: *My love and commitment to her, though, helped me to become a better father and stepfather, to the point where I truly came to enjoy and give to the children in ways that I would never have imagined.* I was moved at reading of this man's struggles to stay in a stepfamily, regardless of the difficulties with his stepson…an invaluable document for couples and parents in stepfamilies."

Dora Capelluto
Stepfamily Association of America

"One of the more realistic and honest books on the market for stepparents. Charles Lund humorously and candidly details his experiences as a stepparent. Certainly a must read for all stepfathers. An enlightening and incredibly insightful read for anyone contemplating remarriage or a stepfamily."

Susan Wilkins-Hubley
Founder: http://2ndwivesclub.com

The Wedding Was Great, But When Does Chuck Leave?

One Stepfather's 20-year Journey

Charles H. Lund

1st Edition

Adams-Bachman Publishing
Oro Valley, Arizona

The Wedding Was Great, But When Does Chuck Leave?

One Stepfather's 20-year Journey

by

Charles H. Lund

Published by:
Adams-Bachman Publishing
1490 E Ganymede Dr
Oro Valley, Arizona 85737-3419
www.weddingwasgreat.com
866-234-4626 (book orders only)

All rights reserved. No part of this book may be reproduced or transmitted in any form or by any means, electronic or mechanical, including photocopying, recording or by any information storage and retrieval system, without written permission from the author, except for the inclusion of brief quotations in a review.

Copyright © 2003 by Charles H. Lund

First printing 2003
Printed in the United States of America

ISBN 0-9727941-0-7

LCCN 2003090305

Cover Photo:
author's stepson-
Erik James Johnson
Age three

To Ilona

*...summoned by consciousness,
I drew near to her and embarked on a journey
of indescribable joy...*

My special thanks to the Stepfamily Association of America for all of the resources that have been so helpful to my family.

I express my deepest gratitude to Dr. Margorie Engel, President and CEO, who, after reviewing my concept for this book, encouraged me to share my experiences as a stepfather.

Chuck Lund

Contents

Forward: **Francesca Adler-Baeder** Ph.D., CFLE

Author's Preface

Chapter I   Page 13

Now Wait Just a Minute

A. The urge to remarry
B. The wounds of the old marriage
C. Who is this new woman?
D. So what's different this time?
E. Do you know her children?
F. Does she know your children?
G. How do you spend your time together?
H. Introversion versus extroversion; a critical variable
I. Your respective worldviews—know what they are
J. So how much waiting is enough already?

Chapter II   Page 33

Brand New Stepfamily—First Adjustments

A. Location, Location, Location—where will you live?
B. Whose children are they?
C. Those "other" parents—how will you deal with them?
D. Grandparents and relatives—double the fun!!
E. Stepparent roles—start on these BEFORE you live together or get married
F. Finances—establish priorities and budgets early
G. Who's the boss?
H. Your values and priorities—honesty is the best policy
I. Three rules for establishing and maintaining a strong foundation for stepfamily life
J. Now that everything's perfect...

Contents (cont.)

Chapter III　　　　　　　　　　　Page 61

Are We Having Fun Yet?

A. "Latency"—those golden years
B. "But you promised!!"
C. That stepdad aint so bad after all
D. Is This How I'm Going to Spend My Youth?
E. Finances? What Finances!!
F. Children and money
G. Heck of a time for a mid-life crisis
H. Revisiting your commitment with your wife
I. World On The Shoulders
J. Humor IS the best medicine

Chapter IV　　　　　　　　　　　Page 91

The Terrible Teens

A. Teen *IS* a four letter word
B. Discipline *IS NOT* a four letter word
C. Role reversals—"I thought you said YOU were gonna be boss!"
D. "Chuck hasn't left yet?" – I thought they liked me
E. My son came to live with us
F. Parental guilt revisited
G. Keeping the romance alive
H. Not the nuclear family
I. Is that a bright spot at the end of the tunnel?

Chapter V　　　　　　　　　　　Page 113

Going, Going, Gone?

A. The first one leaves home
B. Higher education—who pays?
C. You wanted them to be what?
D. "Yours" and "Mine"—the ugly monster returns?

Resources　　　　　　　　　　　Page 121

Forward

by

Francesca Adler-Baeder, Ph.D., CFLE
Director of Family Life Education
Stepfamily Association of America

Professor, Human Development
and Family Studies
Auburn University

I am so impressed with this beautiful story of life, love, mistakes, challenges and hope. Although Charles Lund's story is uniquely his, his experiences are shared in many important ways by stepfathers and stepfamilies throughout the country.

He brings life and humor to the process of creating a family after remarriage. Many men struggle in stepfamily formation since our broader culture offers little in the way of clear roadmaps. His story touches on so many of the issues that we know from research and from clinical work are a normal part of negotiating these unclear family roles and complicated family dynamics.

Rather than a preachy, here's how to do it kind of self-help tale, his is a readable (I went through this in one sitting!), entertaining, and subtle account that will be an enjoyable and valuable resource for stepfathers and stepparents. He offers important lessons learned, seamlessly weaving together stories of personal stepparenting over two decades of family life.

I am most impressed with the honest and thoughtful way he reflects on and explains his thoughts and actions over the years as a husband, as an ex-husband, as a stepfather, as a parent, and as a man, who, through it all, is striving to build a successful, satisfying, and happy life, both as an individual, and as a member of a complex stepfamily.

I am especially struck by the central theme of the love he has for his wife as the motivation to work through the blurry lines of the stepparent/parent roles. The couple creates the stepfamily and his message of building a strong couple relationship in order to build a strong stepfamily comes through loud and clear.

Beautifully written, and powerful, *The Wedding Was Great, But When Does Chuck Leave?* is a love story for our time.

Author's Preface

I present this book to provide comfort, advice and guidelines to men who are members of stepfamilies, and to men who may contemplate becoming members of stepfamilies.

Equally important, I offer this book for wives and moms in stepfamilies who want greater insight into working with fathers and stepfathers on issues such as discipline, finances, relationships with biological parents, and the role of the stepfather with older or grown stepchildren.

I believe that time is a great teacher. This book shares the bumps, bruises, and fun I have had as a man in a stepfamily. Hopefully some of the lessons I have learned may be of help to those who are in earlier stages of their stepfamily journey.

Married at age 23 the first time, I divorced after twelve years. I had two children from that first marriage, Tony and Brian.

At age 37 I remarried. My new wife Ilona, age 34, had custody of her two children, Kari and Erik.

The children were ages four, eight, nine and ten when Ilona and I married. They are all in their twenties now. We had decided not to have any of our own. Although all of the children except Brian lived with us most of the time, Brian was also with us quite often, especially since we strategically located our refrigerator between his house and the school (more about that in Chapter 2).

This book is written from my viewpoint as a father and stepfather. My observations or advice may or may not coincide with the experience or advice of others.

The title of the book, *The Wedding Was Great, But When Does Chuck Leave?* was spoken by a very honest four-year-old. It is not only a true experience, but also a metaphor for all of the good times and the challenges that we have faced in our stepfamily journey together.

Chapter I

Now Wait Just A Minute

"It Is Better To Marry Than To Burn"

St. Paul (Circa 40 AD)

"A Slow Burn May Be Less Painful Than a Hasty Commitment to a Stepfamily"

Ancient Swedish Philosopher (Lund Circa 2003 AD)

A.   The urge to remarry

According to the 1990 U.S. Census, about 80% of divorced men remarried, most within two years of divorce. Of those who remarried within two years, over half remarried within one year of the divorce.

What is the appropriate interpretation of these astounding numbers? Is it that we divorced men have learned so much from our experience that we can stride into our next marriage so soon, and in such numbers? Is this a **macho** thing, like John Wayne leading the cavalry to glory following humiliating defeat? Based on the 45% failure rate of remarriage and almost 70% failure of remarriage when children are involved, a more appropriate analogy might be a horde of **lemmings** rushing over a cliff.

Like many divorced men I have known, I hated the thought of being single, even though there was no doubt in my mind that my marriage was finished. When my wife and I separated, and then divorced, I lost the ability to see my children every day. I lost someone doing my laundry (and reminding me to take out the trash). I lost the sounds and activities of others living with me. As bad as my marriage had come to be, and as irrevocable the decision to end it, the void of being alone felt almost unbearable at times.

And sex! Yes, the loss of sex. Not the "sex on demand" that a counselor claimed most married men had (I have often wondered what planet he and/or his wife were from), but the prolonged absence of any kind of sexual intercourse when the marriage is dissolving, or over. I believe this particular loss can be devastating for many divorced men—it certainly was in my case.

The above statistics demonstrate to me that most divorced men return to the fold of a committed relationship. If my experience is representative, two of the primary reasons very likely are:

- The loss of being part of a family; and
- The loss of a personal and sexual relationship.

I believe that for most men the allure of "swinging bachelorhood" is a fantasy that disappears upon separation and divorce.

In my own case, the first marriage was essentially over several years prior to the separation and divorce. The fact that my wife and I lived together during some extraordinarily acrimonious times was due in no small part to my reluctance to accept the end of the dream of the family, and to my fear of being alone.

B. The wounds of the old marriage

My first marriage deteriorated significantly during the last few years. When my wife and I began our relationship, our very explicit pact was that I would be the strong one, the one who made most of the decisions and provided most of the emotional support. It was gratifying to my male ego, and to my vision of myself, that I would be the captain of the family ship.

When the children came, and when my career started to become intense, my own need for support grew. Her need for support became greater also. I wanted to change the basic structure of our relationship, so that she would orchestrate more and more of the decisions and details of our life. I increasingly resented the burden of her added requirements for support, and often became frightened and angry about the added pressures of children and a career that required more and more of my time and energy.

The inability of my wife and I to continue with the original pact was essentially what ended the relationship. We fought and wounded each other a great deal during those last few years of our twelve-year marriage.

To this day I feel guilty about the fights we had in front of our children. And I've never completely rid myself of the guilt over the lack of time I spent with the children during those early years. My ex-wife and I both worked, and we spent quite a lot of our free time with just each other, or in social situations that did not involve our children. A wonderful woman named Ruth cared for our sons during the day, and also during many evenings and weekends when my wife and I both traveled or were out with friends. Until my dying day I will remember my oldest son's words, *Ruthie is our mother, and you and mom are the babysitters.*

C.   Who is this new woman?

"She'll rip your heart out if you cross her," said a presumably well-meaning employee when I took a job as assistant superintendent at a psychiatric hospital in Eastern Washington.

The reputed woman of iron was Ilona Johnson, secretary to the superintendent of the facility, and assigned to me temporarily until my own secretary could be hired.

Of course the employee was exaggerating, right? However, when Ilona's first conversation with me started with her saying "When you move your family here, you need to be sure to locate in town—I live in the country and it will definitely not be good for your children unless you live in town," I heeded the employee's warning, raised my palms toward the ceiling, and said something like "Who could argue with that?"

Actually, the employee who claimed Ilona could rip my heart out truly deserved whatever heart transplant Ilona might have provided for him, whereas the consensus among most at the hospital was that although Ilona spoke her mind and suffered fools lightly, she was extremely talented and hardworking, willing to help anyone regardless of status or authority in the organization.

Ilona was, and continues to be, forceful, structured, with a strong sense of her own boundaries, whereas I am forceful, almost completely unstructured, and tend to assume that everyone else's boundaries should yield to my own. One of the reasons Ilona and I clicked

18 *The Wedding Was Great, But...*

was that she could more than hold her own with my Sherman Tank personality.

Neither one of us is shy about voicing our concerns. She is at least my equal intellectually, and is certainly the leader of our family in spiritual matters.

From the beginning of our relationship to the present time, we are still learning that we dare not make most pronouncements or decisions without discussing such things with each other first. "Going along quietly" is not a language that either one of us understands.

One of her boundaries has always been that the children, including my children, come first. It took me a while to get used to this, because of course, like most men (or men with childlike tendencies), I wanted to be first. If there was a time conflict between an important activity for one or more of the children, and MY need for *quality time alone* with her, she stood her ground and we scheduled our time alone together for *another time*.

Also, Ilona was, and remains, one of the few people who completely understands my sometimes erratic and abstract thinking process. She not only has a mind of her own—to me she also has a great mind. At times we have discussions where we lose track of time. Of course, in keeping with her character, she is not above telling me "You have obviously run out of things to talk about...but you're still talking..."

Chapter 1 *Now Wait Just a Minute*

D.   So what's different this time?

During my courtship with Ilona, I introduced her to a lifelong friend. He said, "Well, she is certainly completely different from your first wife!!"

As I mentioned earlier, Ilona's personality was forceful. She was not afraid to stand up to anyone, including me.

The two primary differences between my last marriage and my eventual marriage to Ilona were:

- Ilona and I are more evenly matched in temperament; and

- Whereas I had only known my previous wife a few months before marriage, Ilona and I waited almost three years until we married.

My ex-wife is a fine person. She remarried, successfully now for almost as long as Ilona and I have been married, to a man with a temperament much closer to hers.

The forcefulness of my personality was a liability in my previous marriage, whereas it is an acceptable, and even important, asset in my relationship and marriage to Ilona.

I believe that two of the most important factors in the success of our stepfamily experience are what I call ***T 'n T***: *Temperament and Time*. Had I chosen a partner in a second marriage whose temperament was markedly different from mine,

20 *The Wedding Was Great, But...*

there could have been again an imbalance in the "power" in the relationship, leading to a lack of respect by one or both. And, if Ilona and I had not taken the time that we did before we made a permanent commitment, we might not have been able to adequately understand, adjust to, and assimilate the other parts of our relationship that would impact the success of our new family, especially the part of the family that involved the children.

I am not sure if waiting a long time to remarry is a good thing or bad thing in a universal sense, but both Ilona and I were reluctant to move too quickly into a permanent commitment because of the wounding and trauma of our first marriages. Also, although it was obvious enough to know early in our relationship that children from our previous marriages could be part and parcel of a new family, this issue alone would often lead me to believe that **Stepfatherhood is to Fatherhood,** as **Navy Seals Training is to a Cruise in the Bahamas.**

Chapter 1 *Now Wait Just a Minute* 21

E.   Do you know her children?

I believe that taking plenty of time prior to an all-out commitment to a new marriage or relationship is critical when children are involved. Although I did not fully appreciate this when Ilona and I first started dating, it occurred to me as time went on that if I married Ilona, **I would also in some sense be marrying her children.**

As I said earlier, from our early courtship I wanted as much alone time with Ilona as possible. I saw her children (and even my own children) as an intrusion. Many of our "dates" were spent with her and all of the children together. I didn't like it, but I put up with it. Looking back on it now, I would have liked it even less had I re-married too early and then felt trapped in a stepfamily or circumstances that I hated. Time with both Ilona and her children gave me the time to evaluate the prospect of all those years ahead with a new family.

Ilona's seven-year-old daughter Kari was exceedingly easy for me to get along with. Ilona's son Erik, however, proved to be one of the major challenges of my life. Erik was just age two when I first met Ilona; he was nearly five when we married.

Erik had been a great challenge for Ilona also. She and I started dating at a time when, as a single parent, she was still establishing boundaries with Erik. On a scale of 1 to 10 of forceful personalities (with Ilona and I both close to a 10), Erik was a 20. His energy was, and continues to be, phenomenal. And of course I wasn't the "father," so I had to (as was fully expected) bite my tongue. During many of times Ilona and I had planned to be together, I wound up running back to my own apartment, or taking long walks, while Ilona spent time instead with Erik. I often felt that Erik's demanding nature and forceful insistence on Mother's attention robbed me of a great deal of time with Ilona AND her kids. It was hard for me to tolerate massive and constant disruption from a three-year-old.

But I hung in there, and eventually came to actually be in the same room with both Ilona and Erik without feeling disenfranchised or totally resentful at not being able to control or establish limits with Erik. What increased my tolerance as time went on is that I took Erik for treats or tried to do things that he and I both enjoyed (the family dog Buffy was a mutual friend), all the while understanding that **when it came to limits or discipline, I was NOT THE MAN.** I cannot emphasize enough how difficult this was for me.

Over the years this acquired, arms-length mindset of mine came to be a blessing in disguise. For instance, I had often been too intrusive and controlling with my own children— my relationship with Erik helped me over time to establish a more appropriate and supportive relationship with my sons Tony and Brian.

The title of this book, "The Wedding Was Great, But When Does Chuck Leave?" is a great indication of the relationship Erik and I had when Ilona and I married. Even after three years of courtship with Ilona and significant time spent with Erik, the relationship between the two of us was not even close to the father/Ward Cleaver and son/"Beaver" Cleaver stereotype. However, although I did not feel close to Erik (or even that fond of him) at the time of our marriage, I had developed the confidence that I could control my emotions and be part of a stepfamily with him. As for Erik's feelings, his honest four-year-old question **"...when does Chuck leave?"** made Ilona and I both realize that there were many hills yet to climb in that stepfather/stepson relationship.

F. Does she know your children?

Ilona loves children. That's it! End of Story! "Red and Yellow, Black and White, They Are Precious in Her Sight," as my own special version of the old song goes.

From almost the first of our relationship, Ilona knew my children better than I did. From the time she loaned my eight-year-old Tony a sleeping bag to the time just recently she expressed extreme joy over 29 year-old Tony's promotion at work, she has understood, treated, and accepted my children as her own...she needed no decades-long re-training like I did.

Even now two of her best friends are four-year-old and eight-year-old brothers next door. She lets the younger one cheat at checkers (or at least make up his own rules), and she considers one trip or more per month to Target an absolute necessity for the latest and best "stuff" to send my four-year-old niece five states away.

I think her only problem with my children at first, or ever, was really a problem with me—in my attitude, and behavior, I was not willing to set limits with my own children. In time we worked this out.

G.   How do you spend your time together?

As I clarified somewhat already, a significant part "our" time together involved "hers" and "mine," meaning the children. Dining together at McDonald's (in the days before the sound-proof playrooms were added), swinging at the park, "Wee Lambs' Daycare" recitals and bicycle training were all part of the time "together."

Again, this is not the kind of togetherness I envisioned in my perfect world. The tradeoff, though, was being with a woman I adored, who had become my best friend.

From the beginning of our relationship Ilona and I enjoyed talking about religion and politics, two subjects that fascinate us to this day. She was raised Catholic and I was a devoted Baptist well into my college years. Although neither of us had participated in organized religious activities for some time before we met, both of those subjects kept us talking for hours.

From my early twenties I had come to question many of the political and spiritual values that I had embraced as a child and teenager. It was difficult to talk with my immediate family or friends about some of these views, both because they didn't agree with them, and also because some of my views were almost incomprehensible, at times merely questions that formed only a maze of undecided exploration—I found that very few people close to me had any tolerance for such mental meanderings. Not Ilona!! She not only understood and tolerated what I was talking about, but she participated with both intellectual and analytical energy that thrilled me. Our conversations together, and the thrill I get from that, have not diminished to this day. Ilona would sometimes ask, "How are you going to feel about me when I get old and lose my good looks?" My answer has always been, in all truthfulness, "Your mind and temperament are what attracted me to you—the fact that you are beautiful is a bonus."

Children, our children in particular, are of preeminent importance to Ilona. I know that I will never equal her passion in that area. My passion has always been her. My love and commitment to her, though, helped me to become a better father and stepfather, to the point where I truly came to enjoy and give to the children in ways that I would never have imagined—more about that in later chapters.

H. Introversion versus extroversion-- a critical variable

My advice to all anticipating remarriage or any kind of permanent commitment is: understand where you each stand on the introvert-extrovert scale.

It was not until we had been married for some time that Ilona and I realized we had "lucked out" in a very important part of our relationship. We had always taken it for granted that we each mostly preferred being alone or with each other in our free time, rather than with friends, family or in other social situations.

We never thought of ourselves as "introverts"—a term that to us implied some kind of social incompetence. We both have good people skills, very important in the careers we had chosen. It's just that we preferred, and still choose, to spend much of our free time alone or with each other. Neither one of us ever thought of ourselves as "bookish" or "antisocial."

We have known couples who often disagree or even fight about how they each want to spend their free time. "He always wants to have friends over," or "She is always buried in a book and we never see anyone else," are the kinds of complaints that indicate friction regarding introversion/extroversion.

There is a test we have found that removes the stigma of the terms "introvert/extrovert"—the test is merely the simple question, "How do you re-charge your batteries when your energy is down—is it being with other people, or is it spending time by yourself?" If the individuals in a relationship aren't reasonably close in their answers to this question, there can be friction, resentment, or even a loss of interest in the relationship if each is spending too much time apart from the other. This had been true to some degree in each of our prior marriages.

I. Your respective worldviews—know what they are

Holding diametrically opposing views of the world does not mean that a relationship cannot flourish—just look at political consultants Mary Matalin and James Carville, each an ardent advocate for completely opposite ends of the political spectrum. Their love and respect for each other and their children are clear.

If, on the other hand, two people cannot at least tolerate or respect each other's view of the world, there will be trouble. And some relationships with opposite worldviews are pretty much inconceivable, e.g. a man who believes women are inferior in a relationship with a woman who is a strong advocate of the views of Gloria Steinem.

There are possibly as many worldviews as there are people, but it is important to know, outside of the titles, trappings or labeling of such views, e.g. liberal/conservative, what the specific views of a prospective partner are, and whether each partner can live with them.

Because many of my acquaintances and friends became uncomfortable, or even sometimes upset, with my more radical spiritual and philosophical beliefs, I was reluctant to share some of them with Ilona, whom I knew had been a staunch Catholic. On our second date, I took a deep breath and risked sharing some of my more heartfelt, but perhaps unconventional, views about religion and society. To my complete surprise, she not only seemed to understand, without judgment, what I was talking about, but also in some cases expressed similar beliefs.

Even more fantastic, she opened up and revealed an intellectual range and thoughtfulness about the world that led to a three-hour conversation. We had disagreements during that long dialogue, even a first fight. But the flow of ideas was fun, and, for me at least, that second date marked the beginning of our relationship.

J. So how much waiting is enough already?

With some kinds of surgery, weeks and sometimes months are required for recuperation. If something more drastic occurs, such as loss of a limb or the loss of eyesight, the adjustment period can be a matter of years.

The same is true for divorce. Regardless of how negative the relationship has been, it is a severing, or amputation, of a major part of one's life. It takes time to heal, and to learn to cope with being alone and/or responsibly seeking a new relationship.

With a new relationship, if there are children involved, the time required for success in the new relationship is greatly increased because of the enormous complexities of trying to be a family with someone else's children.

For me it has been like learning a new language, **Stepparent-ese**, if you will. And I had not been all that fluent in **Parent-ese** in the first place.

I believe the importance of waiting to make a permanent commitment to a new family is not necessarily to ensure that one becomes an expert in the subject of stepparenting, but to at least be familiar enough with the new job of stepparent to "do no harm," and to understand and cope with any unresolved issues that could lead to another devastating amputation of a family relationship.

In my own case it was a matter of ensuring that I did not lose a relationship with a woman I loved deeply, and of therefore doing what it took to learn and to build the confidence, stamina and flexibility I needed to meet the future challenges of being a stepparent.

The next chapter describes some of those challenges in the first few years of our marriage.

Chapter II

Brand New Stepfamily—First Adjustments

A. Location, Location, Location—where will you live?

In my first marriage the most important goal in my life was succeeding at work. When my oldest son Tony was born I was completing graduate studies, and had been offered a job that promised great opportunities for career advancement. That job, as did others that followed, required that our family move to a new location.

During my first marriage our family moved seven times, for the most part because I was chasing the next great job. The moves were especially hard on Tony, who was eight years old when my wife and I separated. Brian, born two and one half years after Tony, does not have much conscious memory of where we lived, or of the stress involved in all of those moves prior to the separation and divorce.

By the time of my separation, what I thought I had wanted in the perfect career had changed dramatically. Although I had climbed a number of rungs on the career ladder, I found that the higher I climbed and the more I was paid, the more I had to deal with personnel issues, to me much less rewarding and challenging than the staff and planning jobs that had earned me those so-called better jobs in the first place.

A great irony of my separation and divorce was that my focus turned away from my career and toward a very strong desire to have a relationship and a family again.

This need was accompanied, however, by a painful awareness and considerable sense of guilt about the disruption I had created for my family, especially Tony, when we moved so much.

In the years that Ilona and I have been together, my work has continued to be extremely important to me. However, from the beginning of our commitment to each other and to our new family, the priority of my work has become much more balanced with the needs of our relationship and needs of the children, including where we would choose to live, and whether and how often we might relocate.

When Ilona and I first married, she and Kari and Erik were living in a house that she had taken over in her divorce settlement. I was living in an apartment. The four of us established a household in Ilona's house in the weeks following the ceremony. Although the house was in the country, the location to my work was ideal, just three miles away. I loved the proximity to my work, and the fact that the home was located on five quiet, secluded and tree-filled acres. Also, my sons Tony and Brian, who at the time lived with their mother in town, loved coming to the country on the weekends.

However, Ilona had a much longer commute to work than I did, twenty miles to a job she had taken in the year prior to our marriage. Also, providing transportation to day-care for her own children was very time-consuming for her, although I assumed some of that responsibility after we had established a single household.

Soon it became obvious to us that a move closer to my boys and Ilona's work would provide the greatest benefit for the family as a whole, including increased convenience and a greater choice of quality daycare for Kari and Erik. And, although my commute to work would be longer, moving closer to my boys would require much less driving time for me to pick them up for weekends or to participate in their activities during the week.

We consulted with a realtor and gave him a price range and general idea of location for what we wanted in a new home. We told the realtor that we wanted something very close to my sons' elementary school, preferably between the school and their home with their mother. Since my sons were within walking distance of the school and their daycare, this would give them a chance to drop in to be a part of my new family as much as they wanted, and/or as much as their mother allowed.

My ex-wife was quite agreeable to this. She would now have us to help out when she had to work late, or when a babysitter cancelled and she would otherwise have had to drive the boys all the way out to our home in the country.

So, we relocated to what was to be our home for the next fifteen years. Ilona's children now lived in a neighborhood filled with other children, the elementary school that all four children attended was only two blocks away from us, and both of my sons visited frequently after school, if only to see what they could find in our refrigerator on their way home.

Two years later my oldest son Tony, by then age twelve, came to live with us. Although this proved to be quite challenging (chapter IV), our proximity to him during those two years prior had given us much more opportunity to know him, and also gave him ongoing opportunities to become an integral part of the stepfamily prior to living full-time with us.

B. Whose children are they?

Although Ilona and I made a conscious commitment to accept ALL of the children as equally important members of our new family, I found that the process of feeling comfortable as a stepfather was years long, as opposed to a transformation that occurred any time soon after we started living together.

The long-term process of getting comfortable as a stepfather was in many ways the learning of skills that ideally I should have acquired prior to becoming a father in the first place. Such skills included greater patience, and the willingness to spend more time with the children in conversation, play and participation in their activities. A number of my bad manners as a father had gone largely unchecked in my previous marriage, primarily because I had more control as the central figure. In my new stepfamily situation, I had far less control in matters such as discipline, schedule, and activities, a fact that created the need on my part for more patience, diplomacy, tact, and the willingness at times to be more of a helper than a boss.

So, the question of *Whose children are they?* came to be more of a question of *What skills as a father did I need to acquire to become a better stepfather AND a better father.*

The commitment to accept all the children as equal members of the family at times came into conflict with the views of the children themselves. For instance, *You're not my mother*, and *When does chuck leave?* are the kinds of statements that persisted to some degree in the early years of our stepfamily experience.

Also, grandparents, relationships with our ex-spouses, spending on gifts, and who should go on family vacations, were some of the elements that reminded us that our commitment of **HERS** and **MINE** becoming **OURS** was going to be a long-term process.

C. Those "other" parents—how will you deal with them?

When Ilona and I married, Kari and Erik's father was in the military, stationed overseas. This situation continued until the children were grown. So, from the standpoint of day-to-day or week-to-week responsibilities of fatherhood, I was pretty much it. And, because I was their only father within a 3500-mile radius, there were very few visitation issues to work out.

Although the potential for direct conflict between the father and our stepfamily was greatly reduced because of the extreme distances separating us, the impact of this distance on Kari and Erik, and on me as a stepfather, was not altogether positive. For Erik, both Ilona and I had to deal with what I call the "phantom father" syndrome, very much similar to the "phantom limb" syndrome that many amputees experience.

Like the amputee who experiences the illusion that the limb is still there, when in fact the limb is no longer there for support and mobility, Erik sensed that his father was still "there," especially through reminders from the paternal grandparents, who lived nearby. However, unlike an adult amputee who may be able to separate truth from illusion, Erik, as a four-year-old, was lost and confused as to what his "father" meant, especially since he was too young to have had many memories of him, and since his father was not physically there for him to experience directly. In the early years of our stepfamily, it was not uncommon for Erik cry out "I want my Daddy," when he had a nightmare or an injury.

My feelings about this, to borrow an old phrase, were often, *So what am I—Chopped Liver?*

It was not until Erik went to live with his father for a year at age 11 that he was able to develop his own direct relationship. Until that time, he was forced to imagine a relationship with his father through the words of his grandparents or mother, or to try to make more complete sense of the relationship during his father's infrequent visits on furlough.

The title of this section--*Those "other" parents—how will you deal with them?*--for me was a question of *How will I, as a stepfather, deal with the child who longs for a father who isn't there?* From my own personal experience I cannot say if the competition and other problems would have been more or less if Erik's father had been more physically present, but I am reasonably sure that the resolution for Erik could have been much more positive, enabling him to sort out the realities of who is the father/role, and who is the stepfather/role. As it was, both Erik and I were struggling with an invisible, phantomlike issue that could have been more resolvable, if not easier, had the father been more a part of his life. In time, the resolution of Erik's feelings and relationship with his own father allowed the creation of a much more positive relationship between Erik and me.

For Kari, I believe that the primary difficulty with her father living so far away was that there was little chance for a more positive relationship to develop between them. The separation and divorce, as well as some aspects of her prior relationship with her father, had not been positive for her.

However, whatever her feelings were for her father, she seemed far more settled, resolved even, than Erik was about his father. This, together with Kari's laid-back personality and the probability that I was more accepting of her than I was of Erik, helped to create a strong and loving relationship between Kari and me.

D. Grandparents and other relatives -- double the fun

So now my parents had stepgrandchildren and Ilona's parents had stepgrandchildren. From day one all of the grandparents accepted the stepgrandchildren. Their wholehearted embrace of all the children amazed me until I realized that the stepgrandparents were "visitors" who loved children in the first place, and who were actually proud of the fact that they had a larger family, with hardly any more responsibility!

Ilona and I helped all the children to accept the new grandparents as well. The very first time Kari and Erik met my parents, the children ran to them yelling "Hi Grandpa, Hi Grandma."

When Ilona's parents met Tony and Brian, I never had the feeling that her parents looked down on my sons as being less important than Kari and Erik.

Ilona and I both have acknowledged our good fortune in this area. Many of our stepfamily acquaintances have complained of parents displaying less than full acceptance of the new stepfamily.

An illustration of this acceptance includes equal acknowledgement of each of the children by the stepgrandparents at birthdays and holidays. My grandmother, then in her late 80's, was especially meticulous about acknowledging birthdays, holidays and graduations. We wanted to nominate her for stepgreatgrandmother of the year at one point.

There were some other relatives who displayed less than enthusiastic acceptance. Such displays were counteracted with equal force by either Ilona or me, including a few of Ilona's famous open-heart removals.

E. Stepparent roles; start on these BEFORE you live together or get married

Because Ilona and I spent quite some time in our relationship before we married, we were able to establish and test out some of our roles as parents and potential stepparents. This turned out to be especially important in the area of discipline.

Our initial agreement about discipline was that we would each take primary responsibility for the discipline of our biological children. In cases requiring more extreme correction of our children's behavior, we even adopted a "good cop-bad cop" approach, with each of us serving as "bad cop" for our biological children, and as "good cop" for our stepchildren.

In such cases the "bad cop," or biological parent, was responsible for initial discussion with the offender, and for imposition of penalty or corrective action if necessary. The "good cop," or stepparent, was responsible for providing positive emotional support to the offending child without in any way undermining the actions of the biological parent. Our intent was that we would minimize the resentment of our children for each of us as stepparents, while at the same time creating an atmosphere of respect for and adherence to the rules of the household. I believe this division of responsibility between Ilona and me also created an avenue of forgiveness and redemption provided by the stepparent that would have often been much more difficult for each of us as the disciplining parent to achieve on our own.

Our roles in the area of discipline were not without problems, and have required a great deal of adjustment over time. At times we have each had to modify our attitudes and behavior. For instance we were both sometimes more lenient with our biological children than with our stepchildren. And, on more than one occasion we sought professional help when a child's behavior and our respective roles became too complex for us to handle alone.

The time before marriage was important in establishing roles such as "good cop" "bad cop," as well as for establishing positive interaction between us as we adjusted those roles from time to time. Although the time after marriage was a continuation of this same process, we had considerably more confidence than if we had not spent a significant amount of time on such roles prior to our marriage.

Over the years we learned where and when we could modify our roles regarding discipline. For instance, when one of my sons came home wearing a T-shirt with a Megadeath (rock group) skull displayed on one side and a woman without clothes on the other, I was less than forceful about my son's lack of taste and values. Ilona, without prior consultation or approval from me, stepped in and gave her offending stepson the choice of relinquishment of the T-shirt, or banishment from the household.

Another example, this time with one of my stepchildren, was the offender's less-than-contrite response to Ilona about why there had been camping overnight with a person of the opposite sex, and why there had been an elaborate scheme to ensure that we wouldn't find out about it.

> "I lied because I knew you wouldn't let me if I told you," was the stepchild's response.

I thought this was an inappropriate response, given the seriousness of the offense. And, when Ilona imposed the sanction of grounding for three weeks and no attendance at the upcoming prom, the offending juvenile's response was extremely impolite, or at the very least *snotty*. As Ilona had demonstrated in the Megadeath T-shirt incident, I quite immediately and forcefully crossed the boundary of the "no discipline by the stepparent" guideline and assured the offending child that the grounding would be doubled and summer water-ski camp would be cancelled unless compliance and contrition were forthcoming immediately.

In each of these incidents Ilona and I were grateful for the other's involvement.

F. Finances—establish priorities and budgets early.

A professor of architecture once told me that the key to a successful marriage is one bed, one dining room table, and one checkbook.

Regarding the "one checkbook" idea, this is fine in principle, but when there are two incomes instead of one, there can be an illusion of "extra" money unless there is an established budget that correctly forecasts income and controls spending.

Even if the extra money is more real than an illusion, the more there is, in some ways the more confusing it is to set priorities. And, if there is money in addition to the basics, there is also the potential for ongoing disagreements about how that extra money is spent.

In the early years Ilona and I differed about our spending priorities. She preferred spending money on the home and nicer things for the children and me, whereas I liked to spend money on more non-tangible things such as travel, the theatre and special classes.

Ilona was equally generous with all of the children. My problem was that she always seemed to get to the checkbook before I did. Given that we didn't have any structured way to define how disposable income was spent, the children might have great clothes, but sometimes it meant that I couldn't take all of us on a raft trip.

One attempted solution was for Ilona and me to say to each other, "You spent money on your priority, now I want to spend money on mine!" This turned out to be less than productive, because on many occasions we cranked up the credit cards in order to avoid a fight.

We even tried to split the disposable income into two halves, with separate checking accounts. This broke down, however, because in some months there was still the need to pool our "disposable" money for some overall family priority.

We never did resolve this until all of the children left home, because, after the first few years of marriage, the expenses related to food clothing and education, together with the common interest that all of us had for our second home, absorbed all of our disposable income, and then some, especially when the children went to college.

With the children now departed and out of college, and with the return of disposable income (or at least the illusion of such income), we have developed a strict budgeting system so that each of our separate priorities is now negotiated in a very detailed and budgeted income/expense statement prior to the urge to spend. In retrospect this is what we should have done all along.

G. Who's the boss?

In about the third year of our marriage, three of our children were sitting in the living room with Ilona and me, and we asked them who they thought the boss was in family. In unison, they replied,

"Mom"

When Brian, our fourth child, came up from the basement to join us, we posed the question to him. He said,

"Noni's (Ilona) the boss and Dad's the yeller."

When we all got up off the floor laughing, Brian explained that although I huffed and puffed and stormed around a bit about priorities, it was Ilona who actually made most of decisions when it came to all of the children and their priorities.

I said to Ilona, "Do you want to be the boss?"

She said, "Of course—I already am."

I smiled and said, "Good, I think I knew that."

Later, long after all of us had stopped laughing, I reflected on what a change this was from my first marriage. Not that it was necessarily good or bad, but different. And this was much more acceptable to me than having so much responsibility on my shoulders.

This responsibility of "the boss" was due in large part to the ages of our children, and in particular to my reluctance to be involved with them in day-to-day activities. When Ilona and I married they were young children, and I did not enjoy them nearly as much as when they reached their teen years. Ilona, as sort of an "ultimate" mother, delighted in her involvement with all of the details of their lives, whereas many times I couldn't wait to get off and read a book or do something else by myself, or with her.

Over time I became more involved in the decisions about the children, in part because I enjoyed them much more when they were older, and also because over a period of time I began to accept, and even enjoy, my responsibilities as a father and a stepfather.

H. Your values and priorities—honesty is the best policy.

Even though I knew that the children were very important to Ilona, I still held out hope, well into the early years of our marriage, that she and I would be spending significantly more time alone together.

When we were dating she had made it clear that the children's activities and schedules (including those of my own children when they were with us) took precedence over any time we spent just by ourselves.

Her resolve in this area had made sense to me, especially since her priority included my own children. My acquiescence to Ilona's priorities about the children was in large part driven by my guilt about my prior neglect of Tony and Brian.

However, as the weeks and months of our marriage continued, my resentment of her time priority grew, leading to significant friction between us. After one fight she agreed to spend a weekend away with me without the children. It was a disaster.

Following several our fights about this issue, I wondered to myself whether our marriage had been a mistake.

A breakthrough came when we sat down and listed each of our priorities, in order of importance.

Each of our priorities was, in rank order:

CHUCK	ILONA
1. Work	1. Children
2. Ilona	2. Chuck
3. Children	3. Work

What a revelation to me! I had not changed so much after all. With a family and a relationship now in place, my old priority of Work First had reasserted itself.

It turns out that I had been fooling myself into thinking that Ilona was my first priority. When I was really honest with myself, I had to admit that my WORK was again my number-one priority, a condition that I thought had changed for me since the end of my first marriage. What I realized was that I was irritated because I didn't have free access to my Second Priority/Ilona when I wasn't working.

The truth of this became clear when I looked at my schedule. Ilona reminded me about all the times that I had meetings during the evening or was buried in my home office on the weekends trying to catch up with something related to my work.

To me the irony of Ilona's priority ranking was her success at work. By the third or fourth year of our marriage she had been promoted several times and was making more money than I was. By the sixth year she was making significantly more money.

A corresponding irony in my priorities was that, because Ilona's schedule was Eight to Five and mine was substantially unstructured, it fell to me to make sure the kids were transported to the dentist, soccer practice, and otherwise taken care of in their after-school activities.

During this priorities exercise, we openly talked about whether our marriage was viable. She said, with objectivity that astounded me, "Maybe you would be happier with a woman who was ....." I told her, and I was quite serious, that I would rather die first.

The issue of our conflicting priorities still continued, but the fact that I was honest with myself, and with her, helped to lessen the aggravation within me, and to therefore reduce the friction between us.

In the months and years that followed, we devised practical solutions for accommodating each other's priorities, which I will share in later chapters.

I. Three rules for establishing and maintaining a strong foundation for stepfamily life

I believe that three rules, or principles, must be observed in any family, and especially in stepfamilies. Stresses and pressures that can pull a family apart are especially strong in stepfamilies. Such stresses include scapegoating, allowing/promoting arbitrary or non-uniform standards of behavior or privilege, or any other element that does not promote maximum respect for each member of the stepfamily.

These rules are as follows:

1. **Require mutual respect among all members of the stepfamily, as well as among all biological parents, grandparents, or any other person(s) interacting with the stepfamily;**

2. **Ensure that standards of behavior, discipline and privilege are clear, uniform and agreed upon between the parent and stepparent;**

3. **Resolve parental disputes regarding the children in private.**

To elaborate:

1. **Require mutual respect...**

In a training program early in my career, the terms deference and respect were defined to mean: *No matter how you feel about someone, you will not badmouth them, or in any other way*

Chapter 3 *Brand New Stepfamily*

attempt to harm them, either directly or through others.

The training was for my job as a parole and probation officer for the State of Washington. This definition was to be used as a guideline for our behavior as probation and parole officers toward ex-offenders, as well as for minimum standards of behavior that we would expect from the ex-offenders we supervised.

"Deference" and "respect" were cited as minimum requirements for doing a good job with persons who had been convicted of everything from petty theft to murder. Other goals, such as empathy, restoration of confidence, job skills, and discontinuation of criminal activity were important also, but it was emphasized that "deference" and "respect" were the essential building blocks for progress with any of those other goals.

This was a great relief to many of us as probation and parole officers. It meant that did not have to love, or even like, those we were helping. We did not have to be their buddies, or their confidants, although this happened most often when mutual respect was the foundation of the relationship.

For stepfamilies this is a very important principal. Most members of stepfamilies are not petty thieves or murderers, but it is only natural for some personalities and relationships to be quite difficult. In these circumstances, requiring expressions of love or friendship may be setting up such relationships for utter failure and disillusionment, whereas respect, as defined by control of negative behavior, is almost always possible.

56 *The Wedding Was Great, But...*

In our stepfamily we have had our share of personality and relationship difficulties. Case in point: at one time a general condition of hostility between Erik and his three older siblings lead to their burying Erik's Tonka toys and bicycle in the back yard. The bicycle and toys were never recovered (we thought they had been stolen). By the time Erik and Ilona and I learned the fate of the toys eighteen years later, we no longer lived near the scene of the crime. Over the years our insistence upon applying the above definitions of "deference" and "respect" meant that such acts of open hostility became as dead and buried as those old toys.

It is very important to speak out directly to anyone who shows disrespect, whether it is a child, grandparent or other person interacting with the stepfamily. Of primary importance is the need to support a spouse if one's own biological children or relatives are less than respectful to either a child OR an adult. A stepparent can be relatively vulnerable and defenseless with an abusive stepchild (especially in a new stepfamily relationship), in part because there may be insufficient authority or acceptance within the family for the stepparent to directly exercise sanction or control.

Tony was to move from his Mom's home to live with us when he began middle school—he tried to move the timetable up because he told me he resented the relationship between his mother and stepfather. Along with this he flaunted his misbehavior and his contempt of their rules. I told him that he would not be coming to live with us early, because I would not go back on my agreement with his mother. I also told him that unless he demonstrated more respect, i.e. less badmouthing and more compliance with his mom's and her husband's rules, he would not be coming to live with us at all. I applied the same standard to Tony's relationship with Ilona and the other children when he did come to live with us.

On more than one occasion I have been guilty of not speaking out as quickly or as forcefully to a perpetrator when a child, wife or other relative was a victim of another's "trash talk" or negative behavior. There are many ways to say you are not happy with this behavior, but it is extremely important that there is communication to the offender, that such behavior will not be tolerated. I finally said to one such offender, (an adult in this case): "The next time you're tempted to trash...**bite your tongue, and if the negative urge persists, bite your tongue again**—medical help is always available for excessive bleeding."

2. **Ensure that standards of discipline, behavior and privilege are clear, uniform and agreed upon between the parent and stepparent.**

Nothing has more potential for confusion or demoralization in a stepfamily than the ongoing or unchallenged perception that one or more family members are being treated unfairly. For instance, if weekend bedtime is nine p.m. for a twelve-year-old, and weekend curfew is midnight for a seventeen-year-old, the odds are 3.458 to one that the twelve-year-old will try to promote the argument of unfairness. Unless parents and stepparents are mutually agreed and firm about the rules, one or both may be complicit with the argument that the rules are indeed unfair. After all, is there that much of a difference between 9:00 p.m. and 9:30 p.m., mom and dad?

Ninety percent of the issue of fairness is for the parents to have a good idea of what they want to accomplish regarding discipline, behavior, and privilege, set standards in those areas, and stick with them. This is especially true for rules that can be objectified, such as curfew, homework, dating, and children checking in at pre-arranged times. It is also true for discipline or sanctions applied for the violation of those rules, such as grounding or loss of privilege. The rules and discipline in all of these cases need to be as uniform as possible among all stepchildren and biological children, with some adjustments made for age.

Parents in the stepfamily need to set the rules to THEIR satisfaction, ensuring that there is no bias between biological children and stepchildren. Most children will challenge the rules, whatever they are, as not being fair. Ilona and I became quite accustomed to saying, "they may not be fair, but they are OUR rules."

Later in our stepfamily experience, we established a "favorite child" of the month award, a mock reminder that there had never been such a condition.

3. Resolve parental disputes regarding the children in private.

My experience was that the children always seemed to know when I disagreed with Ilona about the way she was doing something with them, even if I never said anything openly. In addition, especially in the early years of the stepfamily, I also made the mistake of disagreeing with her openly about the way she dealt with them. Over time, although we both learned how to "fight fair," even with regard to the children, we came to the conclusion that any of our disputes about the children should be resolved in our own private discussions. There were enough other opportunities for the children to openly see how we resolved our differences.

It is important for the children to see parents resolving differences, to hopefully learn how to "fight fair." What is not advisable is for the parents to try to resolve parental disputes about the children in their presence.

J. Now that everything's perfect...

Of course nothing in life ever reaches perfection. I believe everything we do is mainly to prepare us for another stage of life, which in turn will have its own changes and imperfections. Just as the children grew and changed in their journey toward adulthood, so did my experience and commitment to stepfatherhood change over time.

In the beginning I was not committed to creating an ideal or perfect stepfamily. Rather, my motivation was total friendship and love for Ilona, as well as a good dose of self-interest relating to my biological sons—Ilona was/is a great mom and stepmom.

My relationship with my stepchildren, especially in the early years, was driven by the necessity of getting along. Feelings of joy and fulfillment as the father in a new family were by and large non-existent.

However, as time went on, I became more and more aware of some of the fun parts of being a stepfather, and saw my responsibilities as less of a chore and more of a fulfilling part of my life. I am reminded of the words of a Baptist minister: "Love is an act, not a feeling—love requires no feeling, just the motivation of honoring and respecting others. Everything you do, do out of this motivation and the feelings of love will eventually follow."

For me the "feelings of love...will follow" has been a lifelong process. The next chapter discloses the next phase of my work-in-progress as a stepfather.

Chapter III

Are We Having Fun Yet?

A. "Latency"—those golden years

My understanding of latency is that it is a period in a child's life that is relatively free from the rapid physical or psychological changes that occur in early childhood or in puberty, roughly ages six through eleven.

When Ilona and I married, the children's ages were ten, nine, eight and four. Latency may have been a condition of the children's lives, but it certainly was not a condition of the stepfamily as a whole. For instance, within six months of marriage, we had moved into the neighborhood described in Chapter Two. And, within another six months after that, I had discontinued my fifteen-year employment with the State of Washington to become a management consultant for mental health projects.

So, the children, who by definition of latency were supposedly not going through that much physical or psychological change, nevertheless were surrounded by the major changes of divorce, remarriage, relocation and my career change. Also, my biological sons had experienced a number of relocations of our family before that time.

Whether because of latency, many potential childhood friends in a wonderful neighborhood, Ilona as a mother, or a large house with space for everyone, this period in all of the children's lives seemed to be a very productive time for them. With the exception of occasional scapegoating of Erik, who was considerably younger than the others, the children, almost from the beginning, seemed to enjoy and blossom under the new circumstances. I must say, also, that my own commitment to my stepfamily was different than to my first family. For instance, from assets that I received in my divorce settlement, and from money that Ilona had also, we not only bought a house in a location that was totally beneficial to all of the children, but we also spent a great deal of time and money remodeling and constructing ideal space(s) for them within that house. That kind of commitment, together with a much firmer lock on my tongue than I had had in my previous family, helped to make a much more positive experience for all of the children than it might have been otherwise.

A strong example of our stepfamily success was that the children generally supported each other, even, at times, to the undesirable extreme of covering for each other when one of them got into trouble. And, because we lived in a neighborhood full of children, and because we were in close proximity to my biological sons' home, the focus of the children tended to be away from Ilona and me, and more towards activities like pajama parties, trips with young people's groups, and generally wall-to-wall kids during most of our waking hours.

This period in the children's lives helped me to weather the storm of adjustment I was making in becoming a better father and stepfather. Although the children seemed to be having a lot of fun, in my own heart and mind I was almost mechanically grinding away on my role as a father and stepfather, trying to learn skills of patience and involvement with the children that had never been a significant part of my life before. Also, I was still longing for the day that Ilona would not be so bound up with the children's lives that we could spend more time together.

B. "But you promised!!"

Consistency is absolutely essential for children. In my previous life as a father, I had very little respect for this principle. For instance, if I promised to take the children to the carnival, maybe I would and maybe I wouldn't. Bedtimes, meals and privileges were not consistent or well defined, most often to meet my need for whatever activity was most important to me at the moment.

With the advent of my new stepfamily, I had to learn that consistency and structure reigned supreme. Ilona strongly believed in this principle, and although I agreed with its importance, my old bad habits didn't give up easily—in fact they died a slow and painful death.

Even the time, manner and way that meals were prepared turned out to be more of a ritual than a quick and easy means of obtaining nourishment. I scrambled up some eggs one morning before everyone woke up, thinking that I was going to get the father of the year award. Instead, Kari was extremely disappointed and Erik was furious.

"That's not the way we eat eggs!" Kari said.

"I don't want 'em!!!" said Erik.

Uh-oh. Addicted to change as I was, I soon learned that I dare not mess with the kids' egg habit. They instructed me to 1. Cut out a hole in a piece of bread 2. Butter the bread 3. Begin frying it, and THEN 4. Crack an egg onto the bread hole.

"That's the way you do it," they said.

It was this and countless other incidents that created a number of arguments between Ilona and me.

"You're spoiling the children," I would say.

She would counter, "Just because you're not getting to do what you want every time you want to do it, doesn't mean we're spoiling the children."

Indeed, trips to the doctor, soccer practice, birthday parties at McDonalds or weekend skiing lessons were all priorities that could easily trump my poker night, dinner alone with Ilona, or my attendance at a live boxing match. And, these expectations for activities with the children came with rules about time—there was to be no parental tardiness, let alone cancellation, in either getting ready for these responsibilities, or making sure they happened ON TIME. Tardiness was one of my most treasured sins—giving it up was extremely painful.

I realized, though, all of the times that I had been disappointed as a child because an adult had not come through on some activity or privilege that had been promised.

The year Ilona and I married I promised Tony that he and I would take a week-long backpack trip together across the Cascade mountain range that next year. He told all of his friends about it and had even saved his allowance for camping equipment. It was not until almost four years later that we actually took the trip. Understandably, he was incredibly disappointed.

If this had been an isolated incident, and/or if I had had a bombproof reason for putting that trip off so long, the delay I created would have been more excusable. As it was, my broken promise to Tony was part of a chronic pattern of pushing the children away.

Over the years my sense of guilt about these kinds of incidents has been far more painful than my temporary aggravation at being the chauffeur or facilitator at the multitude of children's events I attended as a stepfather.

Learning from my mistake with Tony, I later took Brian and Erik each on long kayaking and canoeing odysseys at the time I first promised.

C. That stepdad aint so bad after all

In the month after Ilona and I celebrated our sixth wedding anniversary, I took Erik on a six-day kayaking trip, just the two of us on a 100-mile stretch of the Columbia River/Lake Roosevelt waterway. I remember Kari telling Ilona, "After this trip, Erik and Chuck are either going to be best friends, or they're going to wind up killing each other."

As it turned out, the truth was closer to the "best friends" scenario. The warming of my relationship with Erik had actually started during the year prior to that trip.

For almost five years after Ilona and I were married, my relationship with Erik was extremely difficult. For instance, Erik was jealous of his mother's time with me—if he were within earshot of a conversation she and I were having, he would appear, sometimes as if by magic, on the pretext of having something urgent for his mother to attend to.

This jealousy was coupled with the fact that Erik still had a longing for his father. I believe that in his own mind I was still the interloper, unworthy of spending time with his mother, let alone being a stepfather.

Then, in the fifth year of our marriage, Erik traveled to live with his father for the school year. His experience turned out to be wonderful for the relationship between him and me. He got to see that his father was a flesh and blood human being, complete with good parts AND bad parts. And, although Erik and I were not close prior to that time, I had at least strived to "bite my tongue" and not denigrate any part of the meager relationship we already had. So, Erik's unspoken verdict when he returned to our household was apparently (later verified in a more outspoken manner), that I was probably not so bad after all.

Erik came back from his visit with his father with a determination to play baseball. His father had encouraged him in this sport, and had been active throughout his own life in amateur leagues. When Erik returned to our household, he tried out for a local team but was not selected to play. His expectation was so high that he was crushed. He had spent significant time and energy practicing and trying to follow in his father's footsteps.

I knew that Erik had natural athletic ability in some areas. For instance he was already a fairly accomplished snow skier because of lessons and his enjoyment of that sport since he was six years old. Following the rejection from the baseball team, I asked him what he would "really" like to do. He said that he would like to learn how to kayak, and would like to take a long kayak trip. I said "sure," and within two months we were on the trip. During that next year Erik bought a kayak with his own savings, and during the next two years became very accomplished at the sport, including 360-degree rolls under the water and the negotiation of challenging white water rapids. From there he became very proficient at other water sports (including learning how to water-ski on his bare feet), as well as biking and cross-country track. By the time he was in his first year of college, he had totally rebuilt truck engines, had earned a private pilot's license, and had purchased his own plane.

Ilona said Erik would have never been so accomplished if it weren't for me. In reality I had had direct interest in very few of those areas, but I was very supportive, sometimes over his mother's objections, of his risk at trying new things. Some of the detachment I had learned during the rougher years when Erik was younger served me very well—I had no interest in trying to make Erik over into any preconceived image. The discipline I had had to exercise over my own behavior as a stepfather was now paying off, if for no other reason that I was, to use the old medical adage, "doing no harm." Also, I tended to be a risk taker in a number of other areas, and was therefore fully sympathetic of Erik's tendencies in that direction.

With regard to my stepdaughter Kari, the relationship between us was blessed almost from the beginning, although I found that sometimes my aggressive nature was not conducive to an ideal father-daughter relationship. Her manner was extremely accepting, with very little swing in mood or behavior. Her capacity for self-control and deliberation was as pronounced as Erik's impulsiveness and volatility. By the same token, understanding what Kari thinks or feels about something is sometimes a mystery, whereas with Erik there is no question whatsoever.

So I think, perhaps, I earned a passing grade as stepfather to Kari during those first years. According to Ilona, I have always treated Kari as a princess, and am largely responsible for her great self-image. I'm not so sure about that, although my most pronounced memories during that time were my expressions of puzzlement as to why Ilona was so hard on her.

D. Is This How I'm Going To Spend My Youth?

Even though it seemed I was making at least passing grades in the early stages of stepfatherhood, my enjoyment of the job had by no means caught up with my apparent competence. It was as if I were in training for something I was not sure I really wanted to do when I grew up.

So, I was doing a fair job, although I had to take Ilona's word for it many times. But as the months and years went on, the incredible commitment of time and energy to the children, the children, the children, was becoming more pronounced, even if I did at times grudgingly admit that I enjoyed it more and more.

On one occasion I said to Ilona, "Won't it be nice when the kids leave home and we can spend more time together?" Her answer was "Don't get your hopes up, because then there will be grandchildren, and planning for birthdays, holidays with all of us together....."

"Oh great," I thought. "I'm never going to be able to get away from this!"

This was during a time when my flexible work schedule "allowed" me to be responsible for the children after school, including transportation to many of their activities. And, because the children's weekend activities often involved both Ilona and me, it almost seemed I was experiencing **death by children**.

So, I calculated the months and years until they all had their driver's licenses. Wow, I would be in my late forties. My youth would be over. And even after that, with no let-up in Ilona's commitment to them, I would spend the remainder of my life still being an active stepfather. No romantic trysts without the children hanging on, in spirit if not in person. That thought was extremely ugly to me at the time. "What on earth had I gotten myself into?" was the kind of question that dominated my thoughts in the children's pre-teen years.

What kept my commitment strong during that time was my love and enjoyment of Ilona, and the importance to me of a strong family for my biological children. Ilona has often said that if I had not had children to bring into the new family, I might not have been so motivated to stick around. That is a hypothetical possibility that I am now grateful I never had to face.

E. Finances? What Finances!!

At the end of our first year of our marriage I made a major career change, to become a management consultant, as well as to accept a part-time salaried position as a violinist with the Spokane Symphony. Up to that time I had worked for the State of Washington, beginning fifteen years prior as a parole officer, then as a social services planner, mental health administrator and finally as assistant superintendent of a state psychiatric hospital near Spokane, Washington.

The year I made this move we had paid off all our bills, and had established a rigorous budget that supposedly would take care of all foreseeable circumstances. During the first two years or so this worked very well. We met expenses and that was about it.

In some ways the change for me was wonderful. I felt that I had been increasingly locked up in a bureaucracy that was unsatisfying, even though I had been very well paid, including great health insurance and retirement benefits. To become a musician again (I had studied violin on a scholarship at the university level) was like a dream come true, and I could be more assertive in going after consulting work or other part time jobs that could be more rewarding than the constrained activities allowed at my jobs with the State.

In other ways, however, there were great adjustments that I had not fully anticipated. For instance, I had no paid vacation or sick time benefits—if I worked, I got paid; if I didn't, there was no money. So with the freedom came significant anxiety about where the next consulting contract might come from—the salary as a musician made up a relatively small proportion of our family's income requirements.

In addition I now became eligible for the Mr. Mom role. Ilona's job required her to be away from the home from Eight to Five, whereas most of my consulting work could be scheduled any time. (My work as a musician was mainly in the evenings.) Prior to my quitting work for the state we had a live-in nanny for the children who provided care during the day for them when they were not in school. With my career change I was at home a great deal of time during the day to take care of the children, and our budget could no longer support a nanny's salary.

About the third year of my new career I made what to me was a phenomenal amount of money, much more than I had ever made with the State of Washington. Then, rather than continuing with the relatively miserly lifestyle we were accustomed to and budgeting ahead with the new income, we essentially lost the discipline that had been developed earlier. We splurged on a number of things, thinking perhaps that the new income level was a permanent state of affairs.

That year was followed by several relatively lean years, which coincided with significant expenses such as trips to the orthodontist, prom dresses, and illness among Ilona's family that required significant travel and time away from work.

So the freelance life I had chosen turned out to be not so "free" after all. The Mr. Mom role, combined with the uncertainty about income and the ever-mounting expenses, had turned my new bright life into a somewhat uncertain and tortuous existence. Compensating for this was the fact that Ilona was committed to her career, and was rewarded with significant promotions and increases in her income.

During the third year of my new career Tony came to live with us. And while this resulted in a reduction in child support I was required to pay, I soon found out that the money required for food, clothing, school and medical expenses for him was at least as much as I had paid earlier for child support.

Although Ilona received child support from her ex-husband, the amount was fixed and did not adjust for inflation or increased ages and expenses for the children. She could have asked for more as time went on, but she was committed to being as independent as possible from her ex-husband. I perceived that over time the child support she received became less and less valuable, primarily due to inflation and the increasing expenses related to the children as they grew older. Over the years we had heated discussions about this: at times I was only modestly successful in controlling my resentment.

There were several years, especially just prior to the children's teen years, when I felt like I was in living hell. During one time when three children were at home with the flu, I felt like I had come out on the short end of a deal with the devil. I had a tight deadline for a project, funds were tight, but since I was at home, it fell to me to help the children throughout the days they were ill. None of my male background or instincts had prepared me to be the nurturer. During those middle school and early teen years, the kids couldn't drive yet, were not old enough for part-time jobs, and, as they entered middle school years, their natural tendency to rebel against parental structure and authority became more intense. This time of added financial requirements, coupled with my need to be the primary "caregiver" during the day, was further compounded by the fact that, as a stepfather, I was still "earning my wings" as a full-fledged parent for the stepchildren.

Looking back at this time now, I can see that much of what is now an incredible relationship with all of the children came about because I was the Mr. Mom during much of those pre-teen and early teen years. Also, although I was tempted on more than one occasion to go back to more structured employment, I have had a joy and sense of achievement that to me could have never happened in a less flexible environment.

F. Children and money

As the children approached their teen years, we gave them increasing control and responsibility for purchasing their own necessities. With the exception of food, medical expenses, and times out with the family as a whole, a monthly allowance was provided for each of them to use as they saw fit, for clothing, entertainment and gifts they purchased for others, as well as their own personal items. This took the burden away from us for responding to day-in day-out demands or requirements for determining what and how much each of them should have for such expenditures.

As they grew older, they got jobs of their own, which provided even more money for them. Although Ilona and I experienced cash flow pinches from time to time, we kept the children's income for their necessities constant, and tried to keep our money worries to ourselves. We strongly believed that we were responsible for maintaining a feeling of security for all of the children regarding the family's finances.

Where we ran into a problem was how we were to spend our disposable income. Because Ilona and I never developed a plan for times when I earned significant extra income, we essentially spoiled ourselves, including the children, with trips, boats, new vehicles, lots of extra clothes for the kids even outside of their own budgets, and new appliances or personal items for ourselves.

Our approach ensured a sense of financial security for the children, and the assurance to them that we shared our good fortune when there was extra income. What our approach did not do was communicate or instruct financial discipline that would be so important to them as young adults. This had fairly negative consequences later on when they became completely responsible for their own support—more about this in Chapter V.

G. Heck of a time for a mid-life crisis

Both Ilona and I came from families that were less-than-prosperous financially. Both of us found in our early adult lives that we were far more prosperous than our parents had been, both because our levels of education were higher, and also because the standard of living for society as a whole had become greater than when we were children.

For both of us, however, the expectation to get married early was very strong among our families. Also, the expectation I had for myself that was that I would have a secure job that would not change until I retired—my own family's finances were far from secure when I was growing up.

Both my first marriage, as well as my commitment for spending 30 years in the same job, fell apart at about the same time.

During my fifteen-year experience as a state employee, all of my jobs and promotions turned out to be mostly boring to me after the first few months. Frequent promotions kept my discontent at bay for a number of years. Then, in what turned out to be my final promotion, I accepted a position as an administrator at a state psychiatric hospital. For me that job, although paying extremely well and with ostensibly a great deal of responsibility, was boredom personified.

Although I enjoyed the relationships with my colleagues, I felt suffocated in an environment that emphasized politics and keeping things on an even keel. I often complained to one colleague that I needed an MBWA degree for that job—Management By Walking Around.

Compounding my frustration, and later my guilt, about taking this job, was that I had moved my family 300 miles away from our previous home, a move that was very unsettling to all of us, especially my oldest son Tony. My relationship with my wife at that time had been on shaky ground for several years. Six months after the move for the new job, my wife and I separated, further aggravating anxiety and stress among all of us.

Within three years I was married to Ilona, but my dislike for the hospital administration job had only increased. My dream of retiring after 30 years with the same employer became much less important than trying to do something with my life that had more meaning.

I had the opportunity to move back to the state capitol to accept a staff and planning assignment, but that would have meant moving Ilona and our new family away, as well as further separating me from Tony and Brian. And, to me it would have only assured more years of a boring and unfulfilling work life.

So, with Ilona's blessing and a cash reserve, I auditioned for and won a part-time salaried position with the local Symphony, and within a short period of time after that landed a small contract for management consulting.

As I mentioned in a previous section of this chapter, although it seemed after of few years of this career change that I had jumped from the frying pan into the fire, I had nevertheless unwittingly put myself into a position where I, distasteful as it was at times, was able to make a more direct and positive contribution to my children and my stepchildren.

Because of my career change, my time working at home during the day allowed me to have more direct impact and interaction with them. Not only that, but the fact that we now had a location that we were committed to for them gave all of them a great deal more stability for forming friendships, and an ongoing sense of connection and membership in the community. For instance, Erik to this day maintains close ties with other young adults that he has known since kindergarten. Staying in one location, and letting my career gravitate around that, has given me a partial sense of redemption and peace for all of the moving around I had inflicted on my previous family in the name of my career. Also, my career accomplishments since then have been much more satisfying to me than were the fifteen years of my life as an employee of the state.

H. Revisiting your commitment with your wife

In this pre-teen, early teen, so-called latency era, Ilona and I were still sorting out many aspects of our own relationship.

As far as the family was concerned, my time alone with her was my greatest priority, whereas her commitment of time and attention to the children was her greatest priority.

At about the sixth year of our marriage I finally realized that her priority regarding the children was not going to change, at least while the children were at home. And, it was clear to me that another of our priorities were in conflict with each other—in her time off she liked to stay at home and do projects that improved the home, whereas I liked to travel off somewhere to get away from all the home responsibilities.

I came to the conclusion that I would either have to accept her priority regarding the children, or leave. We actually had several conversations where we quietly and openly discussed my leaving as a possibility. I decided that this was not an option for me, and that I would work to change my feelings and my own direction about the children. After all, I could not deny the principle of putting the children first, especially since my own biological children, Tony and Brian, were becoming such a part of the family.

So, at the same time that I recommitted myself to the relationship, Ilona expressed commitment to try to come my way too. Some compromises then took place that surprised both of us as to

Chapter 3 *Are We Having Fun Yet?* 83

how effective they became in bridging our differences.

Early in our relationship we had invested in a long-term lease on a small lake cabin that all of us seemed to enjoy for weekend trips. However, as the children became a little older and had more activities in town on the weekends, Ilona was more and more reluctant to spend time away from our primary home. There began to be weeks or even months at a time when the cabin sat idle.

In the process of discussing our recommitment to each other, we agreed that we could structure the children's lives so that we would spend at least two weekends per month away at the cabin, provided that we planned ahead to be available for the most important children's activities in town. Furthermore, the children, especially as they became teenagers, did not have to spend the whole weekend with us, but would be expected to spend most weekends that we used the cabin, with the provision that they could bring whoever friends they wanted to the cabin on the weekends we were there.

This turned out to be ideal for both Ilona and me. It met her need for staying relatively close to the children. It also met her need for "staying at home," since the cabin became more and more of a second home as we continued to improve it with projects she enjoyed.

The big payoff for me was "getting away," also being with Ilona, and using the cabin as a jumping off place for my own trips, or short trips with the children for hiking, water sports, and day trips into Canada.

Also, marathon, weekend-long Monopoly and Risk tournaments with all of us were now possible, whereas in town there were a great many activities and distractions, including a home office for me that fed into my workaholic tendencies.

Another compromise was that, instead of a number of dates in the evenings, or weekends away by ourselves, we would structure smaller times, such as a walk together to a nearby park, a date having coffee at McDonalds, or a movie together in between ferrying children back and forth to their activities. Because I was gone so much during the evenings and the weekends as a musician, these times became estrmely important to me, and greatly satisfied much of my need for time alone with Ilona.

The balancing act between our priorities, my day-to-day interaction and supervision of the kids, and the unstructured and often intense nature of my own career, were all pressures that became more and more integrated into my life as the children became teenagers.

I. World on the shoulders

During this latency and pre-teen era, because of the way I looked at myself and at the family as a whole, I saw myself as a victim of overwhelming responsibility. I perceived that my personal and vocational priorities were essentially in conflict with what I was actually doing as a stepfather and a husband. I did not see the family as a resource to me, or as an integral part of my life. The stress of this, combined with the fact that I was responsible for significant income for the family, made me feel sometimes like I was carrying a huge load. The picture of a 98-pound weakling carrying a huge globe of the earth on his shoulders became for me the metaphor of what I was feeling at times.

I think this general state of self-pity was in large part because I did not see myself as an integral part of the family, and therefore did not fully appreciate the resource that the family was to me. For instance, I took it for granted that the children often provided valuable help to me in my work, such as ushering at concerts or other events that I produced. Also, I often did not recognize or thank Ilona on the occasions she filled in for me at home because of my work responsibilities.

As the years progressed I began to realize how much the family accommodated to my own life, such as my evenings away as a musician, my ability to work for myself, and the freedom I had working at home. However, the children were well into their teens before I began to actually enjoy the interaction and support from the family as a whole.

J. Humor IS the best medicine.

One of the reasons Ilona said she was attracted to me was because I had a great sense of humor. However, with the family, my impatience tended to predominate over any sense of humor when the children were younger.

The teen years for the kids became my favorite time. By that time I had begun to enjoy and more completely accept the conditions of fatherhood and stepfatherhood.

One of the interactions with the children I had always enjoyed was writing poetry as clues to an Easter egg hunt, or putting the children's toys in odd positions when they weren't looking. I did enjoy the children early on at times like these, but it wasn't until later, when I was starting to enjoy myself more as a stepfather, that I began to consistently share my sense of humor with the family.

For instance, on auto trips our family had some great times naming tumbleweeds that smashed into our car as they blew across the road. A monstrous tumbleweed named Ralph stuck to our front grill until we had to stop the car for refueling. Unfortunately, because Ralph fell to the ground and disintegrated as soon as we stopped, he was unsuitable for mounting on our wall at home. On some trips we slaughtered whole tumbleweed families as they tried to escape over those bleak desert highways. Not one tear was shed for Big Bob, Ophelia or little Jenny.

Another activity that became a family tradition was pretending to recognize people we had never met before. This tradition started on a trip where the family was dumbfounded that I seemed to recognize so many people who should otherwise be total strangers.

For instance, Alicia Proctor came walking out of hotel where we were staying. I was amazed to see her there. She was a lover of mine from days gone by, before I met Ilona, *that's* for sure. When the children and Ilona asked why I didn't approach Alicia, I said it was to protect her privacy, that she probably wouldn't recognize me anyway after all these years, plus any kind of a reconnection with a former lover was certainly going to be uncomfortable for all of us anyway. This sounded perfectly reasonable, but right after that I recognized Chad and his Dad, where the excuse of protecting their privacy grew thin. By the time we passed the Clumpett family—all fourteen of them having lunch in the dining room, Ilona and the children were onto my game.

The increasing frequency of times like these were accompanied by the boys getting bigger and stronger, when they could participate in more rugged sports that I enjoyed, for instance the kayak and hiking trips I talked about earlier. As she became older, Kari, who was born an extrovert, was frequently my date on mandatory social occasions required by my work, occasions that Ilona and I ordinarily would avoid like the plague.

With the children approaching puberty, I was really beginning to enjoy my role as a father and stepfather. By the time the children were in their teens, I was having a great time. They were not so dependent on my time, and the challenges they faced, which largely related to their own issues of independence, were to me merely matters of discipline and family structure. Such matters to me were like a walk in the park compared to my earlier aggravation and lack of commitment to the family as a whole.

While Ilona became somewhat distraught at times because of the children pulling away from us, I felt like I was in my element. First of all, by the time children were in their mid-teens, I had largely earned my wings as an adult authority, making it easier for me to help with discipline during those turbulent years. Secondly, I truly enjoyed encouraging and watching the children spread their own wings.

Chapter 3 *Are We Having Fun Yet?*

Midway upon the journey of our life
I found myself within a forest dark,
For the straightforward pathway had been lost....

But after I had reached a mountain's foot,
At that point where the valley terminated,
Which had with consternation pierced my heart,
Upward I looked, and beheld its shoulders
Vested already with that planet's rays
Which leadeth others right by every road.
Then was the fear a little quieted...

From Dante's INFERNO
(translation by Henry Wadsworth Longfellow)

It aint over 'til it's over

- Yogi Berra -

Chapter IV

The Terrible Teens

A.   Teen *IS* a four letter word

I remember from my own youth that rebellion and turmoil during the teenage years is a fact of life. I thought my parents were stupid then, and I even hopped a freight train one afternoon to prove just how stupid they really were. Of course later that same day, without any concession to their intelligence, I returned home just in time for dinner.

There were at least several patterns Ilona and I had to deal with during our own children's teen years.

The first one was keeping the older children from killing Erik. Erik is six years younger than Tony, five years younger than Kari, and four years younger than Brian. As I mentioned in an earlier chapter, the three older children had buried many of Erik's toys early in their relationship.

"Would you tell Erik to leave me alone?!!!" was more or less a constant theme among all three older children during their teen years. Erik's inquisitive nature, combined with his high energy and yearning for the older siblings' attention, created the need for Ilona and me to be highly vigilant about his well-being. We also had to find ways to teach the older children patience, and to channel Erik's overwhelming energy in other directions.

The second pattern was the children's defiance of our rules. All of the children increasingly tested such parental requirements as curfew, chores, homework, and time with friends. One of our rules was that if a child committed to an extracurricular activity, especially if it involved significant up-front expense and parental involvement, there had to be a bombproof reason why the child would be allowed to withdraw early from that activity. The extreme test and act of defiance of this particular rule was one child (who shall remain nameless) stealing a fifth of whiskey from the liquor cabinet, drinking half of it on the way to school, and then throwing up in the presence of the adult leader of that activity. The discipline for this particular offense will be shared in the next section.

Less pronounced, but still serious, acts of defiance included missing curfew, defacing family property, or getting a D on a report card when all the other grades were A's and B's (the offender in this case said he/she just wanted to see what it would be like).

The third pattern, which Ilona and I saw as by far as the most serious, was each of the children's attempts to avoid, or evade, responsibility for their actions. This included lying to us, failing to report automobile accidents, and attempting to refuse discipline for their misdeeds.

One of the irrefutable laws of the universe is that there is at least a 96.543% chance of a traffic accident occurring within a year or two of a teenager's receiving a license to drive, either because the teenager causes it directly, or because his/her defensive driving skills are underdeveloped. A corollary rule is that, regardless of how many other vehicles the teenager drives, the accident will most always occur in the vehicle of a parent.

Teenagers, regardless of the time in driver's education, parental coaching, or other pre-driving preparations, tend to be unable to realize that they are driving an instrument of potential death, and that driving carefully is just as important as the proper care of a stick of loaded dynamite. To them the 2,000 pounds of potential harm they are controlling is an abstraction until they actually destroy something in an accident.

Ilona and I were never as upset about the accidents as we were about the children's attempts to hide the damage, AND their own responsibility. On one occasion, one of our children had taken a family car out the night before, and had gotten up unusually early the next morning to leave with a friend for school. When I looked out at the driveway later that morning, I saw that the car, which was usually driven to school by that same child, was not drivable.

Later that evening:

Author: "You took the car out last night. This morning I saw that one of the tires was flat and had a gash in the sidewall. How did that happen?"

Child: "I don't know. I don't remember."

Author: "So do you remember or know anything about the long dent in the

> front passenger door, with the green paint and scratches all over the side?"

Child: "Uh, no, not really."

Upon further questioning, the child admitted the damage was probably created when the "car ran onto a concrete traffic median, and sideswiped one of the green signs." I think that this particular response was constructed to help me believe that the car was at least partially responsible for its own damage.

B. Discipline *IS NOT* a four letter word

In the case of this unreported automobile accident, the offender was grounded for two weeks for the accident itself, and an additional four weeks for lying about it. In addition, because the offender tried to hide such a serious offense, television and Nintendo privileges were cancelled for the entire grounding. All of our teenagers subjected us to similar accidents and prevarications, with roughly the same parental response.

The discipline for this kind behavior was far more severe than the punishment for the rebellion involving the half bottle of whiskey described in the last section. We considered disrespect of the destructive power of an automobile, together the failure to take responsibility for the accident, as far more serious than an isolated rebellious act involving alcohol. For one thing, because the drinking and vomiting occurred at school, the child was suspended from school for a week. In addition, there had already been the significant embarrassment and physical discomfort during the trip to a hospital emergency room. Also, even though we were extremely upset about this incident, the school counselors assured us that there was very little likelihood that this type of incident would occur in the future—there was no pattern of other substance abuse, and this, together with the week-long suspension of an otherwise excellent student, meant that we had a very slim chance of ever seeing this type of incident again.

Nevertheless, a grounding of three weeks was added to the punishment from the school—and the counselors were correct; we never saw this kind of behavior from that child or from any of our other children.

Ilona and I agreed that part of the discipline of the children was also a discipline of us as parents. That is, we were to agree as to what was appropriate control and punishment, and to resolve our differences about such matters outside of the children's presence or earshot. We also agreed that our own behavior with all of the children would emphasize positive reinforcement and praise for good behavior, with absolutely no mention of past offenses, unless those same types of offenses reoccurred.

In all cases of teenage offenses with the automobiles, Ilona and I agreed that I would administer the discipline, despite the fact that two of the offenders were my stepchildren. By the time the children were in their teens, I had been more completely accepted as an adult authority by the stepchildren, and also by Ilona.

I believe children at any age are reluctant to accept the authority of a new stepparent. I can see where it could be so much more difficult to be a new stepfather with teenagers than a new stepfather with younger children. Increased control and discipline required for teenagers have the potential of not only isolating the new stepfather from the children more severely than with younger children, but also requiring the mother's greater attention to matters of discipline and control, thereby diverting her attention that much more away from the relationship with the new husband.

C. Role reversals—"I thought you said YOU were gonna be boss!"

Early in our stepfamily relationship, Ilona was the primary disciplinarian, especially with her own biological children. The reasons for this are more fully explained in previous chapters. The primary reasons are 1. I had not yet been accepted as an adult authority figure within the stepfamily, and 2. I had been reluctant to embrace the stepchildren in a relationship in the first place.

Early in their lives, the children needed a great deal of minute-to-minute, day-to-day structure and direction from a parent, and Ilona reveled in that role. As the children began pulling away from parental influence in their teen-age years, Ilona and I often stood on opposites sides of the fence regarding the children's drive toward independence.

The children's pulling-away didn't bother me a bit, but Ilona occasionally had a very hard time with it. To me, the children's independence meant that I had more peace and quiet, but for Ilona it often meant increased worry about what the children were doing out of her presence, and what, where, why and who they were doing it with.

"Kari should have been back by now," she would say at times.

Then, I would likely respond, "Kari still has ten minutes."

We did have strict rules that required each of our children to give us detailed descriptions of their plans when they left the house. This included the requirement that they call us if there were any changes in those plans. Early in their teens we exercised detailed authority over all of their plans. Regardless, I believe the "mom" factor, or what I like to call the "mother hen" factor, caused Ilona to worry. To some degree the worry was understandable: for instance it seems everything Erik chose to do was potentially life-threatening, whether it was rock-climbing, kayaking, climbing Mt. Rainier, getting his pilot's license, mountain biking, or scuba diving.

As the children grew older in their teens, I thought it was important that they had more freedom in choosing what they were going to do, with less monitoring and interference from the parents. Ilona agreed in principle, but when it came to specific decisions, she and I were often in disagreement:

Ilona: "I just don't think it's safe or wise for (nameless teen) to go to the...
Author: "Aw, let 'em go."

My motivation to give the children more rope was not only related to my affinity for "peace and quiet," but also to my own midlife decisions to venture out and take risks. I had been bottled up for most of my adult life with self-imposed constraints related to safety and security—the children's urge to venture out coincided with my own mid-life decision to choose a less secure but potentially more rewarding work life. I could relate to the children in this way and in many cases encouraged them toward independence.

I think it was easier for me than it was for Ilona to sort out what should be the rock-bottom rules for the children. On some occasions when I felt she was being over-protective, she would throw up her hands and say, "Ok Chuck, but it's on your head if anything bad happens." Increasingly, though, she willingly deferred to me on decisions about some unusual trip or event that one of the children proposed.

By the same token, I had no reluctance to impose punishment or control for teen behavior that was deceitful, disrespectful, or that flouted basic rules related to curfew, homework or chores. On most occasions Ilona wanted softer, less severe, sanctions for such behavior than I did.

As the teenagers grew older, Ilona deferred more and more to me in matters of discipline and privilege for the children. My acceptance of the teenagers' drive toward their own independence, together with the stepfamily's acceptance of me as an adult authority figure, lead to, in many cases, a reversal of the earlier roles Ilona and I had played regarding discipline and authority.

D. **"Chuck hasn't left yet?" – I thought they liked me**

There were more than a few times when I overheard one or both of my teenage stepchildren utter derogatory comments about my leadership, choice of clothes, personality, terrible jokes, boring conversation, line of work, or other stepfatherly sins. In these instances, however, I had to admit than such remarks were no different in intensity or frequency than such remarks made by my biological children.

E. My son came to live with us

Tony, my oldest son, came to live with us just prior to his twelfth birthday. He had wanted to come much sooner than that, primarily because he and his new stepfather had been having a great deal of difficulty in their relationship.

Ilona and I had been married for two years, and I welcomed Tony's arrival. I was pleased in the first place that he chose and wanted to live with us, and I felt that since he already knew the ground rules of our household from his frequent visits, the adjustment for all of us would be relatively stress free. He and Ilona had established a respectful relationship, and I, by that time, had become quite insistent on both Tony and Brian respecting their stepmother and following the rules of our household.

The relationship and discipline issues turned out to be not so much of a problem between Tony and his stepmother Ilona or the rest of the household, but between Tony and me. I had been very authoritarian and neglectful of Tony in his early years. Tony's temperament and energy were very much like Erik's. However, in Tony's case, because I had been the central authority figure, I had been unfettered by any restrictions that affect the authority of many stepfathers. The result was that I tended to deal with any childhood issues in my first marriage with overwhelming, and at times excessive, authority.

When Tony came to live with us, the issues he had with authority regarding his stepfather came with him, and transferred immediately to issues he had with me. I then tried to apply the same aggressive discipline I had exercised in the past, including a spanking. To this day I am ambivalent about how aggressive I was in this instance, and soon after Ilona and I instituted a rule that prohibited any kind of corporal punishment, for any of the children.

It took me a while to exercise restraint, patience, and what I thought was the same kind of consideration I had disciplined myself to show Kari and Erik.

Over the next two years, just as I thought things were getting better, they fell apart. Tony increasingly became upset by Erik's attempts to pay attention to him. Erik idolized Tony, but Erik would often refuse to take no for an answer when Tony asked to be left alone. In addition, Tony began to have issues with homework and discipline problems at school. Finally, after Tony expressed fear that when he entered high school, he would lose all of his closest friends, we sought professional help from a counselor.

Ilona and I and Tony, along with Kari and Erik, went to family counseling to give Tony a forum for expressing any of his concerns, and to give us greater insight in our role as parents.

My understanding going into counseling was that none of the issues had to do with me personally. During the sessions, however, it turned out that a great many of Tony's issues did in fact have to do with me, and that we had all needed the help of professional counseling to bring that out.

After one family session, the counselor asked me to talk with her alone. She revealed that Tony had shared with her, in one of their private talks together, that Tony still perceived that I came down way too hard on him, and that I was far too derogatory and aggressive when establishing limits or punishment. She gave me specific examples. After I had confirmed to her the specific facts of those examples, she shared that perhaps my own parental behavior could have been less verbally harsh and aggressive. She suggested that I spend more time with him in activities he and I might enjoy together, and that this might make it easier for him to accept any correction or structures from me, as well as easier for me to tone down the volume and aggressive nature of any structure or issues that I needed to communicate to him.

I was dumbfounded, but was almost immediately grateful for the counselor's help. It turns out that Tony had channeled much of his anxiety about his relationship with me toward issues such as his behavior with Erik, problems at school, and the fear of losing his friends. The sessions and discussion with the counselor led me to realize that the restraint and respect that I had shown toward my stepchildren probably had not been demonstrated to as great a degree toward my own son.

I was far more careful after the sessions. I continued to be strict, and to set limits, but tried to do it in a much gentler fashion. I never relinquished my commitment of establishing boundaries of behavior for the children, as well as escalating restrictions if necessary. However, the discipline and respect that I had had to acquire for my stepchildren made me that much more receptive, and I believe capable, of eventually modifying and softening my direction with my sons Tony and Brian.

F. Parental guilt revisited

It was fifth year of our marriage when the talks with the counselor took place. The realization that I had a lot more work to do on myself as a father to my own sons came at a time when I was beginning to feel quite a bit more comfortable with my role and performance as a stepfather.

During this time, and ever since, I have often felt sympathetic towards advocates of reincarnation, especially toward those who believe that the work we did to improve ourselves in this life helps to ensure that we will start out at a higher level in the next life.

During the children's teen years, although I was experiencing greater confidence, enjoyment and skill in my role as a stepfather, I realized that my opportunities to be a better father to my own sons were now limited to their few remaining teenage years. There was no way I could go back and start over. Also, I felt that all of the work I was doing to improve myself in being a better father would be almost equivalent to someone retiring just after graduating from trade school, with little or no chance to apply the new skills. Hence, I began to understand and sympathize with those who believed that acquired skills could be carried over into a reincarnated life.

During the children's teen years, the relief I had long felt at the thought of all the children being grown and gone was increasingly replaced by my guilt that I had blown my opportunities as a father, and would have little further opportunity to apply the fruits of repentance—my western mind could not take the total leap of faith toward full acceptance of progressive reincarnation.

Chapter 4 *The Terrible Teens*

Ilona, aware of my feelings during this time, reminded me that I was not, and had not been, the only actor in the boys' lives. Their mother, for instance, had been, and was now, equally responsible for my sons' nurturing and development. Ilona's argument created little comfort for me, and in fact increased my confusion; I felt incapable of evaluating my ex-wife's competence, or the lack thereof, in light of the divorce and the trauma that had been created for my sons and the family as a whole.

For instance, guilt about my boys created the "should my ex-wife and I have stayed together or not?" obsessions, along with "would it have made any difference?" speculations. The circular nature of these thoughts created significant exhaustion for me. Finally I came to the conclusion that, regardless of what might have been done differently, the fact was that those days were dead and gone, and that I had to deal with the guilt of that irrevocable fact.

This guilt that reared its ugly head so forcefully during the children's teen years has never completely disappeared. Perhaps this is somewhat akin to the death of a child, in that the feelings of longing never completely disappear, even years after the child has died. The truth of that analogy is something I hope I never have to experience directly.

Even though I was mostly great at setting and enforcing limits with all of the children, my guilt during their teen years at times made me less direct with my own sons than with the stepchildren. But this was not often, and when it did happen, Ilona provided me with strong reminders about my responsibilities in this area.

G. Keeping the romance alive

Ironically, the more my attention shifted away from Ilona to the family as a whole during the children's teen years, the stronger my relationship became with her. I'm sure part of this increasing harmony related to less conflict about my trying to pull her away from the children. Also, I think that as I became more involved with the children, Ilona and I had more in common for discussion and relationship during the times we were alone.

Neither one of us has ever had an affinity for sunsets, moonlight dining, walks along the beach, or cruises in Tahiti. Although she always says I have spoiled her rotten with gifts, attention, and various tokens of affection, her idea of maximum romance is our working in the yard together or doing projects around the house. Although she denies it, I think she would have had great success as a pioneer woman.

And she doesn't like surprises. I made the mistake early in our relationship of surprising her with a birthday party with all of our friends, or with an unannounced night on the town. Even surprises for the family as a whole were not the way to win her heart, unless *she* had advance notice. As Yogi Berra might say, **"She doesn't likes surprises unless she knows about them ahead of time."**

I have a friend who, when he pulls into the garage, always puts his hand on the hood of his wife's car to see if the engine is warm. He knows that her trips outside the house are stressful for her, and that it takes her awhile to readjust once she returns. Likewise, I have learned that Ilona

Chapter 4 *The Terrible Teens* 107

is happiest when everything is part of a routine, including when we go to movies, when we go shopping, when we call the children, and when and how I'm supposed to do my part of the housework.

For me, routine is death. If I do anything in the same way more than once or twice, I get bored or, in extreme circumstances, feel that my life may be coming to an end. Fortunately, where Ilona is not routine relates to one the most important parts of my life, and our life together. That is, she is very well read and is able to tolerate, and even enjoy, the way I change my mind all the time about political, social, philosophical, or all other issues that do not pertain to our personal life and schedule. Her capacity for discussion and intellectual exploration has kept me fascinated with her for all these years. And, to be totally honest, I appreciate the fact the house is clean, all the children's birthdays are honored, and dinner is on time, even if some of this requires my routine participation.

There is an old saying, that 80% of success is showing up. In keeping the romance alive in our marriage, my success has been almost 100% related to 1. Demonstrating respect for our family as a whole, and 2. Making sure the trash gets out to the curb before the truck comes in the morning.

H. Not the nuclear family

In a long-extinct TV series, a baby dinosaur often rejected assistance from the dinosaur father, with protests of "Not the Mama, not the Mama." Similarly, my early experiences as a stepfather were accompanied by spoken, as well as unspoken, sentiments of "Not the Father. Not the Father."

Shortly after Erik's historic question of "When Does Chuck Leave?" he began calling me Dad, probably about the sixth week after our marriage. Ilona had told him, in the best language a four-year-old could understand, that I wasn't going anywhere. (She also told me, in no uncertain terms, that Erik was NEVER going anywhere.) However, for many years, I was "Dad" in name only, in my own mind as well as in Erik's.

Sometime during the stepchildren's teenage years, in their eyes I believe I had achieved at least equal status with their father, as an authority figure as well as a parent who was respected and loved. However, despite this very positive track, until they were grown I never completely lost detachment and wariness about the children's father or their biological grandparents, aunts and uncles. The litmus test I projected was that if anything ever happened to Ilona, would there still be a relationship with the stepchildren? I feared that the answer would be no.

Most of the stepchildren's paternal relatives lived nearby, and continued to have a very good relationship with Kari and Erik, as well as a pleasant if somewhat reserved relationship with

Ilona and me. The children spent time with them and with their father when he was on leave from the military. One summer both Kari and Erik were away for three months visiting their father, and Erik spent an entire school year with his father during his fifth grade.

In truth there was no longer a nuclear family for the children, or for Ilona or me. Our divorces from our previous families created yet other families that continued to be very important for all of us to deal with in a positive way. Our awareness of and sharing the children with those families, while not as difficult as the process for my acceptance of the initial restrictions of stepfatherhood, were yet another stress and outside condition that, in my own mind, pulled in the opposite direction of our stepfamily becoming a cohesive unit.

As opposed to my earlier tendency to push the children away, I was somewhat resentful of ANY involvement by these families during the children's teen years. After all, my skills and privileges as a parent to my children and stepchildren had come at great price. I began to empathize with the feelings Ilona had had about my own boys from day one.

I eventually came to accept the truth that all of the families were important. To me the various family units are similar to a binary star system. We all revolve around each other; and, regardless of the size or importance of any family unit at any given time, we each will hopefully continue to have a positive impact and relationship with all of the children.

I. Is that a bright spot at the end of the tunnel?

Earlier in my life as a stepfather I fantasized about the time the children would all be gone, grown up and independent financially. My theme song when things got especially stressful was Roy Clark's old hit, "Thank God and Greyhound (They'll Be) Gone." Even Ilona, great mom that she was, sometimes spoke of the days, especially during the teen years, when the children would be "out of sight, out of mind."

By their late teens, the children had established a pattern of decent grades, good manners (for the most part), a great work ethic in part-time jobs, and a sense of responsibility toward themselves, each other, and the outside world. The rebellion of the earlier teens had largely disappeared, and increasingly we only saw them only for obligatory family times, or for when they had to do their chores. During the last part of each of their senior years, we came within a whisker's width of eliminating curfew, but pulled back for the simple reason that Ilona was not able to sleep unless she knew the children were safely home.

My attitude and sense of responsibility as a stepfather had improved greatly over the years. With this came a greater enjoyment of all of the children and a desire to actually be with them more often. However, as much as their respect for me had improved, often the last thing they wanted to do was to spend time with *The Dad*. I remember that the last time I was able to get Erik and all of his friends over for pizza and penny-ante poker was in his fifteenth year, and I had to practically bribe them all to do it.

Chapter 4 *The Terrible Teens*

Earlier in my stepfatherhood I saw my existence as equivalent to the analogy of that famous dark tunnel, where one keeps trudging along with the expectation that if one sees a bright spot, it will signify a breakthrough to light and freedom, rather than the headlight of an onrushing locomotive. In those early years, I saw the bright spot as the time when the children would be out of the house.

By the time the children were in their mid to late teens, I noticed that although the bright spot of their departure was still quite a while down the road, the dimensions and livability of my "tunnel" had improved dramatically. I actually missed them when they weren't there so much. Conversations with them when they were at home tended to gravitate toward sharing the latest jokes, getting them to commit to a time when they could come away with us for the weekend, and planning the next, and increasingly non-obligatory, family vacation. Compared to my relative enjoyment during this time, Ilona hated the teen years. She fretted that she was losing control, and that the children no longer needed her in their day-to-day life. She adopted Roy Clark's old hit as her own theme song during the kids late teens, whereas I would increasingly think of the tune "Aint No Sunshine When (They're) Gone." I was no longer able to see any bright spot at the end of the tunnel, because for me the tunnel itself had become a pretty bright and happy place to live.

112 *The Wedding Was Great, But...*

We've Only Just Begun

- The Carpenters -

Chapter V

Going, Going, Gone?

A.   The first one leaves home

The tunnel became a little darker for me when Tony left home to start his freshman year in college. Not darker in the sense that it felt like the drudgery of my early years as a father and stepfather, but darker from the standpoint that I now, to a great degree, had lost any further direct opportunities for atonement with him for earlier fatherly shortcomings. The darkness also increased because of the fact that I would miss him as a day-to-day part of the family.

The expenses for his support would increase, because we had committed to assisting him, and all the children in their turn, with their college tuition as well as room and board. The level of financial support for all of the children would became substantial over time, as Erik would not graduate until ten years after Tony started his freshman year. To be totally honest, the thought of the financial responsibilities ahead darkened the tunnel a bit further for me.

Ilona and I and Kari helped Tony to move into his dorm room at school. Kari and Tony had become especially close during their high school years—she helped him pack for school, and, in the style ala Ilona, gave him very specific instructions on where she thought things should go in his dorm room.

To say that Tony seemed nervous when we all took him to school is an understatement, and reminded me of the time I took him to school on the first day of his first grade. I remember that time long ago as if it were yesterday—desk by the window, third row from the front of the class. I especially remember my feelings of helplessness as that small boy nervously explored his desk and tried to find a place for his pencils. In some ways I felt no less helpless as we said goodbye to Tony at the university, even though we had celebrated his nineteenth birthday several weeks before his classes were to begin.

I remember that the strongest feeling I had at that time was tremendous gratitude toward Ilona for embracing Tony as one of her own children. In some ways Tony could be as abrasive and demanding as I was—I think he learned a healthy respect for Ilona, and for women in general, because of her constancy, and also because he knew, despite how tough she could be at times, that he and the other children were first before me, first before her work, and first before her own life. In a conversation with Tony a few years later, I shared with him that I was dead certain that Ilona would give her own life for any of the children in the split second she perceived such an action would save any of them. He said, in a tone as serious as I've witnessed in Tony, "I know that."

B. Higher education—who pays?

When Tony went to college, his mother and I had an understanding that I would continue to support Tony, and that she would continue to support Brian through his college years. So, Ilona and I provided the only financial support Tony was to receive from parents for college. Both Tony and Brian earned four-year degrees; their mother turned out to be true to her word in helping Brian with college.

When Kari and Erik went to college, there was no support from their father. In fact his child support ended for each of them at their high school graduation. It had been a matter of principle for Ilona that she would never ask her children's father for increases in child support, nor for assistance with their college expenses.

Early in our marriage, whenever Ilona tried to explain her rationale for not taking her ex-husband back to court for the children's support, I had tremendous difficulty understanding her reasons. My attitude was "Get the Guy." For one thing he was so far away that Kari and Erik were with us every weekend, whereas my ex-wife had every other weekend "off" when Tony and Brian came to visit. It crossed my mind that perhaps Ilona was going easy on her ex-husband because she felt some kind of misplaced sympathy for him, or guilt that the family was no longer together.

These semi-paranoid ideas of mine could not have been further from the truth. Although I never did completely empathize with her reasoning, I at least understood it. She wanted to ensure that her ex-husband had limited control or leverage of her custody or raising the children. Her decision to pursue her career was also in keeping with her desire to be as independent as possible in her support for her children.

I had to admit, that, when Tony went to college, Ilona never said anything about the imbalance of support for him. In fact, because she was making more money than I was at the time, and because all of our money was in one pot, in effect she was paying proportionately more for Tony's college than I was.

My acceptance of Ilona's decisions and control regarding her ex-husband's financial support has been almost as important to our relationship as my acceptance of her lifelong commitment of putting the children first. Such acceptance was especially important, because our financial support of the children did not end with college. As the children tried to spread their young adult wings after college, there were times of overwhelming expense to them, mostly borne of mistakes and inexperience. Some of these mistakes related to our less-than-adequate job of preparing the children for their own financial responsibilities as adults.

C. You wanted them to be what?

One of the rules we had for the children was that, when they graduated from high school, we would help to support them financially if they went to a two-year, four-year, or vocational training program, but they had to live on campus, even if they went to a school within commuting distance of our house. And, if they decided not to go on to school, they had to move out of the house and find a job and support themselves. Another rule was that they had to be matriculated on a full time basis—we would only support them if they took a full load of classes. And, with that full load, they had to achieve high enough grades to avoid academic probation.

We wanted all of them to have at least some kind of higher education. We also wanted to discourage them from living at home in an undecided state. We felt that if higher education or living at home/working at McDonald's were the choices, they might decide to extend their childhood longer than we would have liked. Furthermore, since Ilona turned into a basket case in each of the children's senior year, any of the kids living at home beyond high school would have surely put her in the funny farm.

Tony and Erik went to college gladly. Tony had always wanted to attend the University of Washington in Seattle. And, although Erik wanted to be a pilot (he was well on his way toward getting a commercial license when he entered college), he also wanted to have a degree where he could earn a living if he were not able to pass the pilot's physical at some time in the future.

For Kari, however, these rules had unintended consequences. After almost two semesters of lackluster, and very expensive, academic performance, she expressed to us that what she really wanted to do was to move across the state to Seattle and get a job. Kari's reluctance to have been forceful about what she really wanted was, in part I believe, related to her knowledge that we would be happiest if she were in school earning some kind of degree. In addition, there would have been no financial support from the parents for what she *really* wanted to do.

Kari did move to Seattle toward the end of that first year after high school graduation. Almost immediately she got a full-time job as a nanny, earning almost as much as a trade school graduate. She had always been gifted with children. She did so well in fact that she was hired at a very good salary by a couple who worked at Microsoft. The couple kept her on for seven more years, and has since included Kari in many of their family activities. As of the writing of this book, Kari is working as a nanny for another wonderful family. Along the way she has earned a college degree, has traveled all over the world, and is pulling down a better salary than many college graduates.

We are proud of all of our children and their work ethic. If I had it to do over again, I would have not expressed such bias toward higher education, and I would have offered more help for children who just wanted to establish themselves right away as working adults. We did help Kari quite a bit when she decided to move to Seattle, but it would have been more productive and helpful if we had made that option available to her in the first place.

D. "Yours" and "Mine"—the ugly monster returns?

By the time the older children were adults, out of college, the ugly monster of "yours" and "mine" had disappeared. The most prominent feeling and activity I can remember is that if a problem occurred with any of our young adult children, I could easily turn into "Dad on a mission."

I welcomed my turn to be "Father Hen." When either Kari or Tony had a problem with auto insurance, moving to another apartment, help with resumes, co-signing for loans, Ilona and I were both there to help, with our time and with our financial assistance if necessary. I can recall how vulnerable I had been when I was supposedly all on my own. And even for Brian, although I was technically not financially responsible, there were opportunities to lend a hand there as well.

Ilona or I could have been resentful of the children's added need for support during these times after college, especially if it were a "stepchild." That didn't happen. And, in the time that has passed since then, Kari, Tony and Brian have made increasingly wise decisions about their personal and financial decisions. The need for our support in those areas has largely disappeared.

The children have been very helpful to me also. Kari, for instance, was a great morale booster at a time when there were difficult publicity challenges for one of my contracts. And Tony seems to be the first one to read, comment and help with any part-time writing I am doing.

What is very gratifying about the disappearance of the monster is that it is nowhere to be seen near any of the children. All of our children are in contact with each other frequently, in person, by phone, letters, or trips to see us.

Just one month prior to the writing of this section our son Brian called. I wasn't at home at the time. When Ilona picked up the phone, the first thing she heard was "Noni, you're going to be a grandma in 2003." He didn't say stepgrandma. He said grandma. Wow.

Ilona and I both can truthfully say that the terms "biological children" and "stepchildren" have now totally lost their meaning for us. They are all our children.

And Erik? That four-year-old who was so anxious to see me leave is now a 23 year-old who graduated from college this past year. He and I talk about once a week when he calls us on our toll free 1-800 number. He has his first full-time job now, as a bush pilot in Alaska. We invariably end our conversations with:

> "Take Care. Love you Dad."

> "Love you too, Erik."

Resources

Stepfamily Association of America (SAA) – The Stepfamily Association was founded in 1977 by stepfamily research and practice pioneers Drs. John and Emily Visher. The Stepfamily Association of America was incorporated in the fall of 1979. It has since grown into an active national association comprised of people and organizations from across the United States, Canada, and other parts of the world. In summary SAA is:

- A nonprofit organization funded by memberships, sale of educational resource materials, and donations.

- A national association of people concerned with helping stepfamilies live successfully.

- A network seeking to change attitudes about stepfamilies through advocacy, media coverage and solid research.

- A provider of education, training, and support for stepfamilies and professionals who work with stepfamilies.

Stepfamily Association of America
650 J Street, Suite 205
Lincoln, NE 68508
1-800-735-0329
www.saafamilies.org

Your Stepfamily Magazine - A bi-monthly magazine created by SAA for all members of a stepfamily—to help them grow, learn from and enjoy the relationships they're creating together. www.yourstepfamily.com

Stepfamily Solutions - offers individual, couple, family and group counseling for stepfamilies. Workshops and classes provide training to mental health professionals and organizations. http://www.stepfamilysolutions.net

Stepping Stones Counseling Center - created with the goal of improving and enriching the quality of stepfamily life and experiences. http://www.stepfamilies.com

The Second Wives Club - A comprehensive, interactive site touted as "the online haven" for second wives and stepmoms! http://www.secondwivesclub.com

Building A Successful Stepfamily - Designed for Christian stepfamily couples, those considering remarriage, and single parents. They teach keys to healthy stepfamilies, to promote strength and wisdom in meeting the challenges of stepfamily life. www.swfamily.org/stepfamily

Smart Marriages - A resource-rich national clearing house for premier educational and support programs for couples. www.SmartMarriages.com

The Children's Foundation – a private non-profit organization founded to improve the lives of children and those who care for them. www.childrensfoundation.net

Children's Rights Council - A national nonprofit organization based in Washington, DC that works to assure children have meaningful and continuing contact with both their parents and extended family regardless of the parents' marital status. http://www.gocrc.com

The Stepfamily Network - a nonprofit organization dedicated to helping stepfamily members achieve harmony and mutual respect in their family lives. http://www.stepfamily.net

StepCarefully for Stepparents - an organization created by stepparents, for stepparents. They offer on-line support, as well as a to-the-point series of resources for step-parenting needs, and a newsletter designed to help stepfamilies survive and succeed. http://www.stepcarefully.com

WIFE - The non-profit Women's Institute for Financial Education provides financial education and net-working opportunities to women of all ages. www.wife.org

Stepmothers International - SAA's Web site provides educational material and support resources for all women and persons who are, or have been stepmothers, stepfathers or in a stepfamily as a stepchild or otherwise related to a stepfamily environment. http://steptogether.org

Stepmom's House – provides a place to visit and to interact with other stepparents. http://www.geocities.com/heartland/meadows/1731

Bride Again Magazine - The only magazine designed for the encore bride. Quarterlies cover issues, both psychological and material, that meet the unique needs of the thousands of women planning to walk down the aisle again. www.brideagain.com

A Stepmom's Haven – provides a private support community for stepmoms, run by stepmoms. Offers weekly group chats, several online message boards, a password protected venting board, and online one on one communication with the managers and members. http://communities.msn.com/AStepmomsHaven

American Family Therapy Academy - AFTA is a non-profit organization of leading family therapy teachers, clinicians, program developers, researchers and social scientists, dedicated to advancing systemic thinking and practices for families in their ecological context. afta@afta.org

Single and Custodial Father's Network - a nonprofit organization dedicated to fathers who meet the challenge of custodial parenthood. http://www.scfn.org/index.html

National Fatherhood Initiative - a non-profit, non-partisan, non-sectarian national civic organization founded in 1994 to stimulate a society-wide movement to confront the growing problem of father absence, and is dedicated to improving the well-being of children by increasing the number of children growing up with involved, responsible, and committed fathers. www.fatherhood.org

Father 4 Kids - information about, and referrals to, attorneys and other professionals who understand fathers' issues, and effectively represent the interests of fathers and children in family court in all jurisdictions.
http://www.fathers4kids.org

American Coalition for Fathers and Children - dedicated to the creation of a family law system, legislative system, and public awareness, which promotes equal rights for ALL parties affected by divorce and the breakup of a family, or establishment of paternity. http://www.acfc.org

United Fathers of America - the goal of United Fathers is to provide an interactive medium for people experiencing the effects of dissolution, parenting arrangements and other family law issues. Secondary purpose is to provide information and resources in the aid of Internet Legal Research. http://www.ufa.org

National Center for Fathering - inspires and equips men to be better fathers. They conduct research on fathers and fathering and develop practical resources to prepare dads for nearly every fathering situation. www.fathers.com

Divorce Central – provides support and communication with others who are in various stages of decision-making.
http://www.divorcecentral.com

Beyond-Divorce.com - topics related to divorce, single parenting, remarriage, and stepfamilies. www.beyond-divorce.com

Divorce Info - designed to help with transitions related to divorce. http://www.divorceinfo.com

Divorce Net - State by State resource center dealing with various divorced family and stepfamily issues. http://www.divorcenet.com

Divorce Online - a resource for people involved in, or facing the prospect of, divorce http://www.divorceonline.com

Divorce Source.Com - offers State-specific divorce information and stepfamily issues. http://www.divorcesource.com

Divorce Support - offers support with divorce, child custody and family law. http://www.divorcesupport.com

Dad's Divorce Rights - experienced attorneys help fathers with litigation and negotiation strategies while always focusing on what is best for the child(ren). http://www.dadsrights.com

DivorceInteractive.com - a comprehensive divorce resource with survival tools, information and helpful resources for divorce. http://www.divorceinteractive.com

Adams-Bachman Publishing

Quick Order Form on Reverse Side
for

*The Wedding Was Great,
But When Does Chuck Leave?*

Quick Order Form

Postal: Adams-Bachman Publishing
1490 E Ganymede Dr.
Oro Valley, AZ 85737

Or: Toll free 1-866-234-4626 (Have your credit card ready)

Or: Order online over a secure server At: www.weddingwasgreat.com

For postal orders, please fill out the following information, make check or money order payable to Adams-Bachman publishing, and mail to the above address.

Please send me ____ copies of The Wedding Was Great, But When Does Chuck Leave? at $12.95 per book. Add 8% if you live in Arizona.

Name: _____

Address: _____

City: _____ State: _____ Zip: ____

Telephone: _____

Email address: _____

Shipping by air:
US: $4.50 for the first book and $2.00 for each additional book.
International: $10 for first book, $6 for each additional book (approximate).

Adams-Bachman Publishing

Quick Order Form on Reverse Side
for

*The Wedding Was Great,
But When Does Chuck Leave?*

Quick Order Form

Postal: Adams-Bachman Publishing
1490 E Ganymede Dr.
Oro Valley, AZ 85737

Or: Toll free 1-866-234-4626 (Have your credit card ready)

Or: Order online over a secure server
At: www.weddingwasgreat.com

For postal orders, please fill out the following information, make check or money order payable to Adams-Bachman publishing, and mail to the above address.

Please send me ____ copies of The Wedding Was Great, But When Does Chuck Leave? at $12.95 per book. Add 8% if you live in Arizona.

Name: _____

Address: _____

City: _____ State: _____ Zip: _____

Telephone: _____

Email address: _____

Shipping by air:
US: $4.50 for the first book and $2.00 for each additional book.
International: $10 for first book, $6 for each additional book (approximate).

Adams-Bachman Publishing

Quick Order Form on Reverse Side
for

*The Wedding Was Great,
But When Does Chuck Leave?*

Quick Order Form

Postal: Adams-Bachman Publishing
1490 E Ganymede Dr.
Oro Valley, AZ 85737

Or: Toll free 1-866-234-4626 (Have your credit card ready)

Or: Order online over a secure server
At: www.weddingwasgreat.com

For postal orders, please fill out the following information, make check or money order payable to Adams-Bachman publishing, and mail to the above address.

Please send me _____ copies of The Wedding Was Great, But When Does Chuck Leave? at $12.95 per book. Add 8% if you live in Arizona.

Name: _____

Address: _____

City: _____ State: _____ Zip: _____

Telephone: _____

Email address: _____

Shipping by air:
US: $4.50 for the first book and $2.00 for each additional book.
International: $10 for first book, $6 for each additional book (approximate).